D0716363

DYNAMO

THE BOOK OF SECRETS

DYNAMO

THE BOOK OF SECRETS

A Beginner's Guide to Modern Magic

BLINK

bringing you closer

Published by Blink Publishing
3.08, The Plaza,
535 Kings Road,
Chelsea Harbour,
London, SW10 0SZ

www.blinkpublishing.co.uk

facebook.com/blinkpublishing
twitter.com/blinkpublishing

Flexiback – 978-1-911600-40-4
eBook – 978-1-911600-63-3

All rights reserved. No part of the publication may be reproduced, stored in a retrieval
system, transmitted or circulated in any form or by any means, electronic, mechanical,
photocopying, recording or otherwise, without prior permission in writing of the publisher.

A CIP catalogue of this book is available from the British Library.

Designed and illustrated by davidjpitt
Cover designed by Steve Leard
Cover illustration by Chris Malbon
Cover photograph by David Ellis
Text written with Andi Gladwin & Joshua Jay

Printed and bound in Italy

1 3 5 7 9 10 8 6 4 2

Copyright © by Inner City Films Ltd, 2017

Steven Frayne writing as Dynamo asserts their moral right to be identified as the author of
this Work in accordance with the Copyright, Designs and Patents Act 1988.

Every reasonable effort has been made to trace copyright holders of material reproduced
in this book, but if any h   ·rs would be glad

Blink Publ   ɔup

DÚN LAOGHAIRE- RATHDOWN LIBRARIES	
DLR27000008532	
BERTRAMS	19/01/2018
GDAN	02311194

STOP!

Before you go any further, visit my website

www.dynamomagician.com/secrets

and use the password '   ' to receive a special
message just for you!

@dynamomagician

CONTENTS

CONTENTS cont

INTRODUCTION

Every effect I perform begins as a dream – an impossible idea that I can see in my mind's eye. Those dreams become my sketches and words in books like the one you're holding. This journal is, quite literally, where my magic meets reality. The very best of these ideas get developed into some of the effects you might see me do on television and on stage. Even the biggest stunts begin on pages like this one.

For this project, I've created a book that I hope will inspire you to practise and perform magic. I have shared 30 powerful effects, and if you read between the lines, there are even more secrets to uncover.

I have purposely chosen effects that are powerful but entirely easy to do. Nothing in this book requires years of work (although the more you put in, the more you'll get out), and you won't get blisters from practising these effects (that has happened to me many times over the last 15 years). Instead, I have chosen magic that will intrigue audiences and allow you to focus on the most important part of a magic show: the presentation.

I'm serious about this

Don't be fooled by my casual style on stage and on camera. What I say is as calculated as what I do. That's why I have provided detailed instruction not only on how each effect works, but the script for each one, and how to prepare in advance for every effect. You'll learn how to make a borrowed ring move without touching it. You'll be able to look through someone's body. I'll show you how to predict the future and know the decisions someone will make before they know. You'll be able to make a chosen card vanish from the deck and appear in your shoe. And later in this book you'll even learn a way to perform a piece of magic on someone with me; I'll actually be there to help you do the magic.

I've also provided the kind of helpful advice I wish someone would have whispered to me when I began – how to cope with nerves, what to do about hecklers, how to put together a show and more. This is exactly the resource I wish I had when I was starting in magic.

Reading someone's book of secrets is like stepping inside their head… so, welcome to my mind.

"Dynamo"

London, June 2017

Exposure?

Magicians aren't supposed to reveal their secrets, right? That's true — I keep many of the effects in my repertoire so secret that I haven't told anyone how I do them. But the pieces in this book are different. I have picked effects that are perfect for people new to magic to learn because they are easy to do, yet get great reactions. There is a world of difference between teaching magic and exposing it and I am teaching these effects because they are the perfect starting point to a life (or even career) in magic!

CAN YOU KEEP A SECRET?

Over the last 15 years, magic has changed my life. It's enabled me to travel the world and see places I could only have dreamed about when I was younger. It's given me the confidence to do things that I never thought possible and allowed me to meet many of my heroes. But ultimately, it's taught me a lot about myself.

This journey started with a single secret… when I was 12 years old my grandpa amazed me with a piece of magic where all of the matches completely vanished from a green matchbox. I begged him to tell me how it worked but he just smiled and said… 'It's a secret, Steven!' For months I pestered him to tell me how it was done but he refused to give up the secret.

Eventually, I started to learn magic myself; I devoured every magic book I could get my hands on and practised relentlessly. While all the other kids were out playing, I was locked in my bedroom trying to master a sleight or a vanish, failing over and over again.

My grandpa never told me the secret to the matchbox trick. Despite all of my success I still don't know the answer to this seemingly simple piece of magic. But it taught me a couple of valuable lessons – firstly, that the simplest of things can be the most amazing, and secondly, that the real magic lives through your ability to keep a secret!

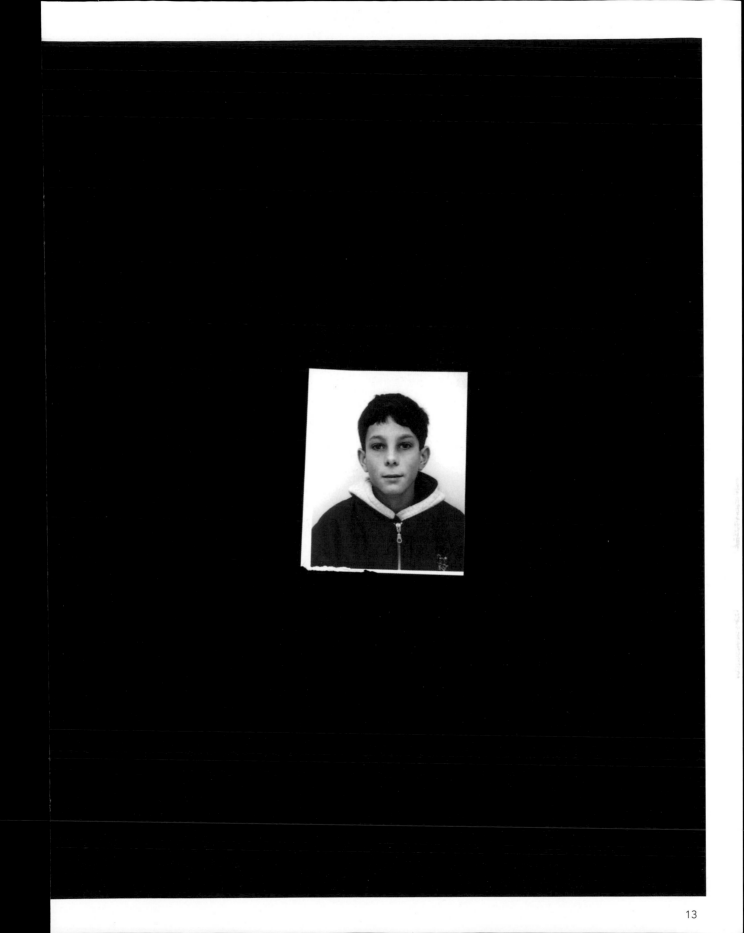

THE OPENER

One of the most important moments in a magic show is the beginning, the 'opener.' So before you dive into my book of secrets, I have something for you, right now. The effect uses something of mine and something of yours. It uses my name – not Dynamo, but instead my real name: Steven Frayne. Notice that the letters of my name form a large letter 'd,' which is what my friends call me for short.

Now we need something of yours. Think of any number between 5 and 20. Got a number? Good.

Place your finger on my face at the top of the design. Then count down, moving one letter for each number. Count the S as one, the T as two, the E as 3, and so on.

As you move from letter to letter, continue in a clockwise direction in a circle. Don't go back up the straight line; simply continue going around the circle.

Now your finger should be on a random letter, and it's a location I couldn't possibly know. To reinforce your thought-of number, I want you to count to the number again, but this time in an anticlockwise direction. Move one letter on the count of 1, and then continue in this fashion until you have counted to your secret number. Now you're on a new, random letter.

Turn to the next page and I'll read your mind.

STEVEN

FRAYNE

PART 1
THE BIRTH OF A MIRACLE

This is your first step in the creation of a miracle: a moment of profound, unexplainable magic that will leave your audience awestruck!

The following effects are both simple to learn and incredibly powerful when performed in the right way, so take your time and practise both the handling and performance until they feel natural (this may take a while, so stick with it!).

As with every effect in this book I've included some scripting but it's important to note that this is only a guide and you may find a better way of communicating the effect that suits your style and character

Basics
Before you jump into the effects, let's take a moment to understand some of the fundamentals about magic and this notebook.

There is no difficult sleight of hand in these pages, but you will still need to understand some basic terms and positions.

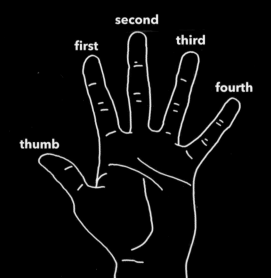

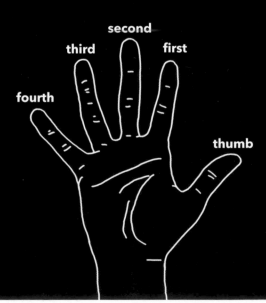

Glossary

Flourish
This is a fancy way of shuffling or cutting the cards. Flourishes look hard, and often are!

Force
This term describes the illusion of a free choice, when in fact you 'force' a participant to select something predetermined. A 'card force' gives the illusion that any card can be chosen, when in fact you know in advance exactly which card the participant will choose.

Force Card
This is the term used for the specific card you will force on a participant.

Gimmick
This is a prop that looks normal but has been altered or prepared in a secret fashion.

Mentalism
This branch of magic is concerned with reading minds and predicting thoughts.

Method
This is the secret way an effect is accomplished. Every magic effect has a method.

Participant
The spectator or spectators who actively participate in your performance. These are the people who pick cards, or take part in the magic.

Reset
This is the time and procedure required to put an effect back into its starting position. You must 'reset' many effects before you perform them again.

Spectators
The people who watch your magic but do not actively participate.

'AND ABOVE ALL,
WATCH WITH
GLITTERING EYES
THE WHOLE
WORLD AROUND
YOU BECAUSE THE
GREATEST SECRETS

ARE ALWAYS HIDDEN
IN THE MOST
UNLIKELY PLACES.
THOSE WHO DON'T
BELIEVE IN MAGIC
WILL NEVER FIND IT.'

ROALD DAHL

FINGERTIP MIND READING

EFFECT
You are able to correctly identify which finger a participant chooses. Better still, you can perform this effect for everyone in the room at the same time.

It's rare to find a magic effect that everyone can participate in, whether you're in a theatre of a thousand people or just performing for a friend. But this is just such a miracle. Despite having your back turned (or even performing the effect over the phone), you perfectly guess which finger the entire audience have selected.

OVERVIEW
Although you give everyone an opportunity to choose a different finger through a series of fair steps, mathematically they can only end up on their first finger.

PERFORMANCE
1. 'If you'd like to help with this next piece,' you begin, 'then put your hand in the air.' Hopefully all or at least many of the spectators raise their hands. 'Wow, that's a lot of you. I'll tell you what. You can all help with this effect. The only thing you need is your right hand, so hold it high in the air. Move your right hand so that your palm is facing you.' Hold your own palm toward yourself as an example, and make sure everyone is holding their hand properly.

2. 'Everyone straighten all of your fingers. Your right thumb should be to the right and your pinky to the left. With your left first finger, point to your right little finger.'

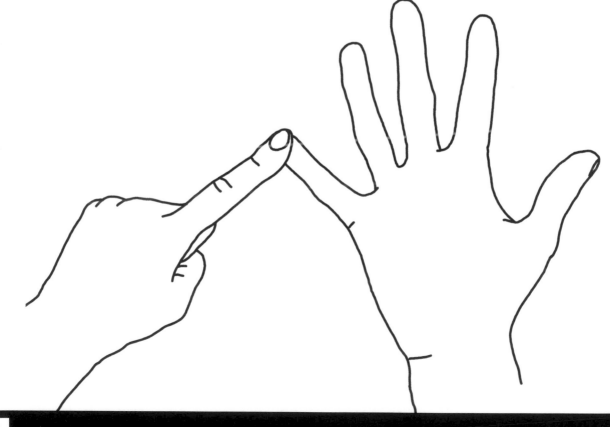

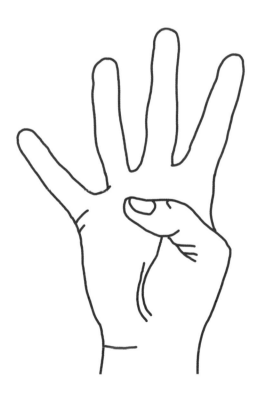

3. 'You're going to make five moves, moving from one finger to another for each move. For this effect only, your thumb counts as a finger, so you can move there, too. You can move left or right, but don't skip over any fingers, so you can't jump from pinky to thumb.' Demonstrate with your own hand, touching each of your right fingers in a series of moves, to the right, to the right, then perhaps to the left, and then to the right again. 'I'll turn my back while you do this because I don't want to see where any of you end up. Go!' Count aloud for them to move once on each number. '1...2...3...4...5'

4. Allow the participants to make five moves, and ask each of them to keep their left finger on the right finger they have landed on. 'You all moved in different ways, so many of you will end up on different fingers. But I am getting the sensation that nobody is left on the thumb, so fold that down. It's eliminated.' Hold your right hand above your head so that the participants can see your hand but you can remain turned away from them. Demonstrate what they should do by folding your right thumb in toward your palm.

5. 'And I'm also getting a feeling that you aren't on the pinky. So fold that down, too.' So saying, fold down the little finger of your right hand and ask them to do the same. These steps are amazing to the participants because it feels so fair. Yet mathematically, it's impossible for them to land on either the little finger or the thumb.

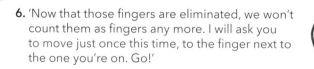

6. 'Now that those fingers are eliminated, we won't count them as fingers any more. I will ask you to move just once this time, to the finger next to the one you're on. Go!'

Although this instruction also feels quite free, the participants have no choice but to move to the middle finger.

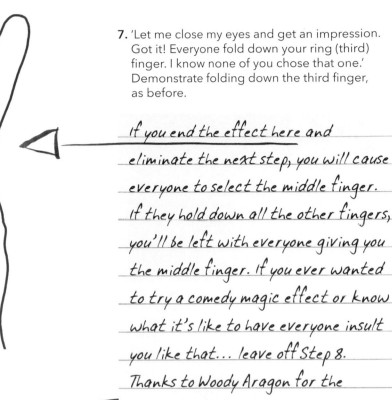

7. 'Let me close my eyes and get an impression. Got it! Everyone fold down your ring (third) finger. I know none of you chose that one.' Demonstrate folding down the third finger, as before.

If you end the effect here and eliminate the next step, you will cause everyone to select the middle finger. If they hold down all the other fingers, you'll be left with everyone giving you the middle finger. If you ever wanted to try a comedy magic effect or know what it's like to have everyone insult you like that... leave off Step 8. Thanks to Woody Aragon for the comedic addition.

8. 'I'd like you to make just one more move. Move to the finger next to the one you're on.' There is only one place for everyone to move here: the first finger.

9. 'Fold down the middle finger because you didn't pick that one. I believe you're thinking of the first finger. If I got it right, hold up that finger above your head.' At your show, everyone will be left with fingers pointed in the air. You read everyone's mind.

WITH THANKS TO: Jim Steinmeyer has created some of the world's most impossible illusions. He is most famous for his large-scale illusions, but I found this effect in his book SUBSEQUENT IMPUZZIBILITIES.

NERVES

Young magicians often me the same question: 'What's the secret to stop getting nervous before performing?' You want to know my secret? I get nervous, too! Not for every effect or even for every show, but I do get nervous sometimes. The key is to channel your nerves into positive energy. Turn those knots in your stomach into enthusiasm for the audience.

There are two other ways to deal with nerves. The first is to have supreme confidence in your material. I rehearse for more than two hours almost every day. I know what can go wrong in every effect in my show, and how I can react to each problem to fix it. Being prepared allows me to be calm.

The second way to deal with nerves is to perform… a lot. There's no shortcut to experience, but after enough repetitions, I feel comfortable onstage, even if I'm sharing a moment with an arena full of people.

H2OOO○○

EFFECT
Reveal a participant's chosen playing card by causing the label on a water bottle to transform before their eyes.

There is often a secret connection between magic and science, and that is what's happening in this effect. The secret is a scientific principle called <u>change blindness</u>. The concept is that your spectators don't notice a small but important change during the effect. You ask them to read the label on a water bottle. A moment later you switch the label, yet nobody will notice – until you point it out.

Search this term online and check out the UNBELIEVABLE clips ... they're like magic!

OVERVIEW
The secret of this effect is printed on this very page! I've designed a special wrap-around label for a water bottle that you can cut out from my notebook and stick to a water bottle. When one side of the label faces your spectators, it will look like a normal bottle of water: Scottish Highland Water, to be exact. But when it's twisted 180 degrees, the colour, design and logo appear the same, but the words change to 'Seven of Diamonds'.

You will use a card force to influence your participant to choose the Seven of Diamonds. Before I get into the explanation, let's construct the prop.

NEEDED:
- A pack of cards
- A normal-size water bottle
- The special label on this page

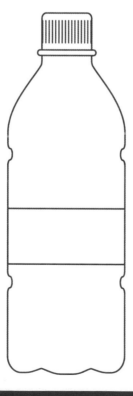

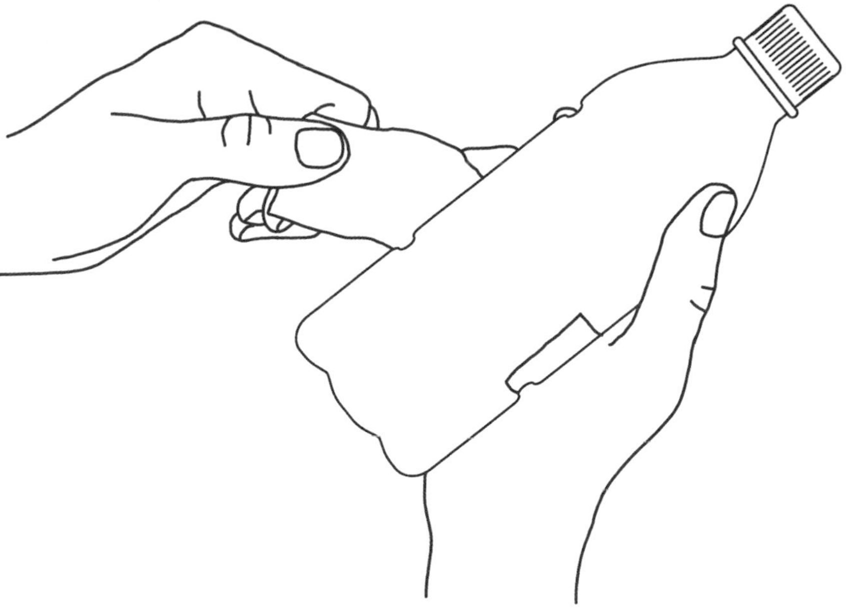

SET-UP

1. Begin by tearing off the label on your water bottle.

2. To prepare the label, cut out the label printed on this page. With glue or double-sided tape, stick the label to the water bottle and trim away any excess paper.

   The two logos should be on opposite sides of the bottle. From one direction, the bottle appears to be from the brand Scottish Highland. From the opposite direction, it will reveal the Seven of Diamonds.

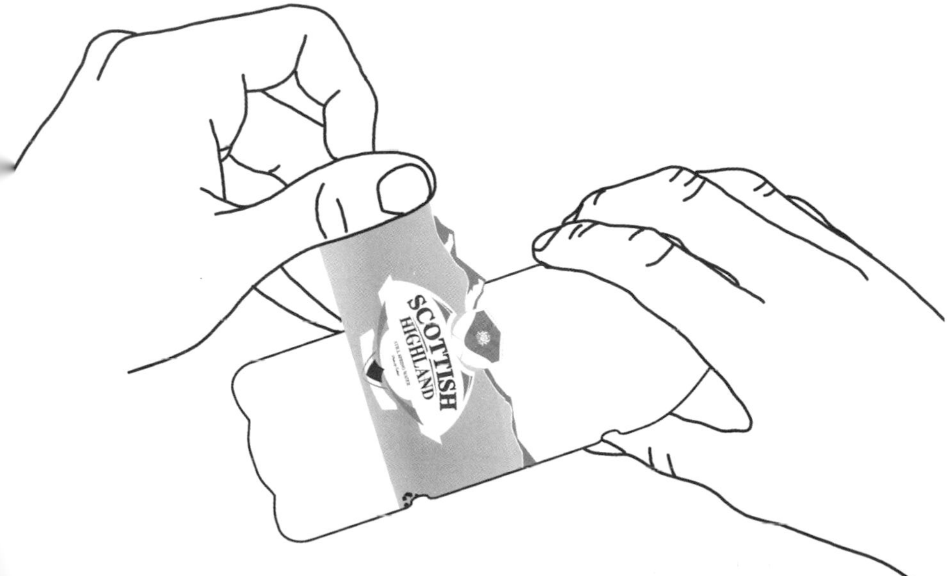
SCOTTISH
HIGHLAND

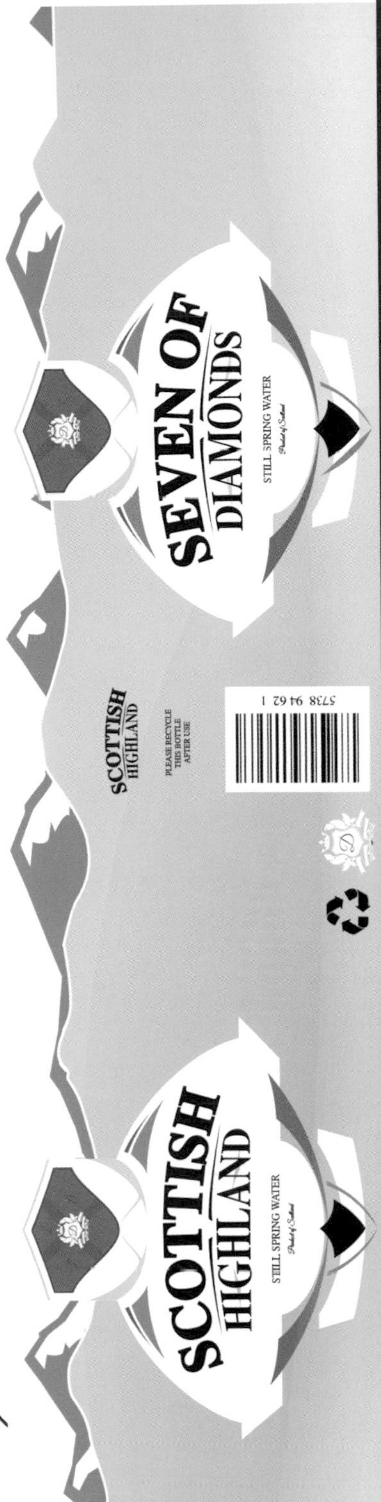
SEVEN OF
DIAMONDS
STILL SPRING WATER
SCOTTISH
HIGHLAND
PLEASE RECYCLE
THIS BOTTLE
AFTER USE
5738 9462 1
SCOTTISH
HIGHLAND
STILL SPRING WATER

3. Before you start the performance, secretly place the Seven of Diamonds on top of the deck. When you perform the effect, casually bring the water bottle into view, placing it on the table to your right. Take care that the Scottish Highland side faces toward the spectators at all times. If you are doing some other effects first, have the water bottle on the table and casually drink from it so your spectators get used to it being there but make sure you're always being careful to avoid the Seven of Diamonds side showing prematurely.

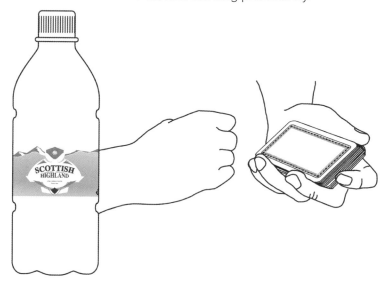

PERFORMANCE

1. 'I'd like you to cut the deck anywhere you like,' you say as you spread through the cards to show that they are different and mixed up. 'I'll place them on the table and I want you to cut off a portion and place it over there.' Put the cards face down on the table.

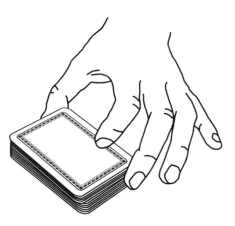

2. Allow the participant to cut anywhere they like and place the cut-off portion next to the lower half of the deck.

3. 'I'll mark the place where you cut by placing the cards like this.' As you talk, pick up the lower portion of the deck and place it perpendicular on top of the packet just cut by the participant.

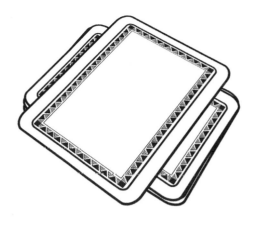

This sneaky procedure is called the Cross-Cut Force. You do honestly mark the place cut by the participant, but by placing the packet in this configuration, it becomes almost impossible to follow precisely which cards came from where. So, in a moment, you will be able to pass off the original top card of the deck, the Seven of Diamonds, as the card they cut to. Watch how it works in the next step.

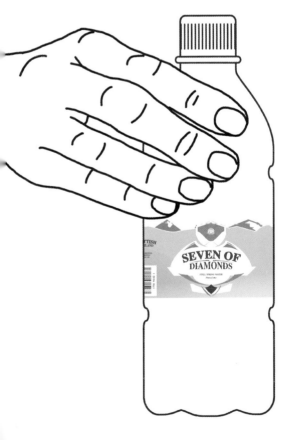

4. You need to pass some time before you can complete the Cross-Cut Force, so that the spectators forget the sneaky placement of the packets. To do this, you will now introduce the water bottle. 'I can't find your card yet because I don't have the power. To get the power, I'll take a quick sip of what looks like ordinary water but has magical powers.'

Now you continue, 'Read the brand of water on the label.' They will read 'Scottish Highland' and you confirm this is the mysterious water that allows you to see into people's minds. Put the top back on the bottle and place it off to your left, but as you do, secretly rotate the bottle so the Seven of Diamonds side is facing toward the spectators. Immediately focus attention back on the deck, and away from the water bottle. Nobody will notice the label has changed – yet.

5. 'Please remember the card you cut to.'
With your left hand, steady the upper packet of the deck. With your right fingers, pick up the top card of the lower portion. This is the force card, the Seven of Diamonds. Hand it to the participant and ask them to show it around and then to mix it back into the deck.

6. 'I see your card is a red card. It's a Diamond. The Six of – no! It's the Seven of Diamonds!' As you reveal the participant's card, stare into their eyes and really concentrate, as if you're reading their mind. When I do magic like this, I actually convince myself I do have the power to read minds in that moment. This is the only way you can achieve an authentic experience, and a great reaction.

7. 'You know how I did that?' Your audience will be eager for you to tell them. 'It's in the water!' Gesture toward the water bottle and build up the effect.

'You cut the deck anywhere you wanted and remembered the card at that position. And you read the label of my water bottle. Do you remember the name? That's right! Scottish Highland Water. Look again.'

Allow the spectators to discover that the words on the bottle have morphed into their chosen card. Toast the audience by taking one last sip of water, and as you pick up the water bottle, cover the 'Highland' logo with your hand and then walk away like a boss.

WITH THANKS TO: The Cross-Cut Force used in this effect is attributed to Max Holden. It's a great force, and we'll use it again later in this book.

I was lucky enough to sit down with Teller (of the legendary magic duo Penn & Teller) in London, and he reminded me of the importance of honesty in magic (which may seem strange when discussing an art often associated with deception). Teller is a true master of the art (I don't say that lightly) and, despite being a man of few words, is one of the most inspiring magicians I've had the pleasure to meet.

MARTIAL ARTS MAGIC

EFFECT
Borrow a banknote from a friend and immediately stab your finger through it! Then cause the hole to heal like magic.

When I started in magic, this was one of my favourite effects to do for strangers on the street. It takes about ten seconds to perform, is easy to do and can be performed with a borrowed banknote.

OVERVIEW
For a split second, you will disguise your second finger as your first finger, and this helps create the illusion of one fingertip going through the note.

NEEDED
Any borrowed banknote

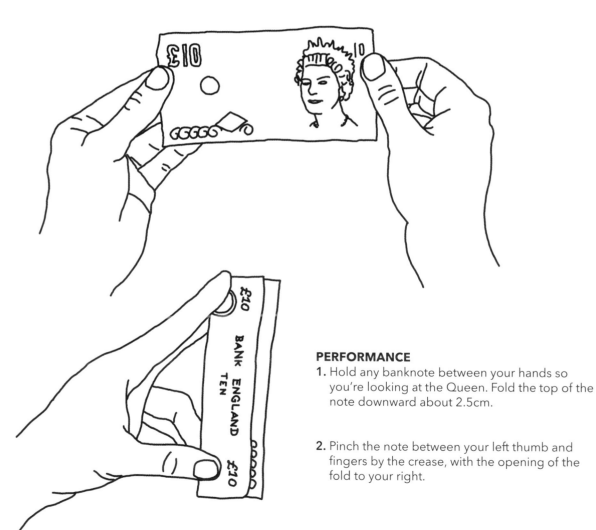

PERFORMANCE
1. Hold any banknote between your hands so you're looking at the Queen. Fold the top of the note downward about 2.5cm.

2. Pinch the note between your left thumb and fingers by the crease, with the opening of the fold to your right.

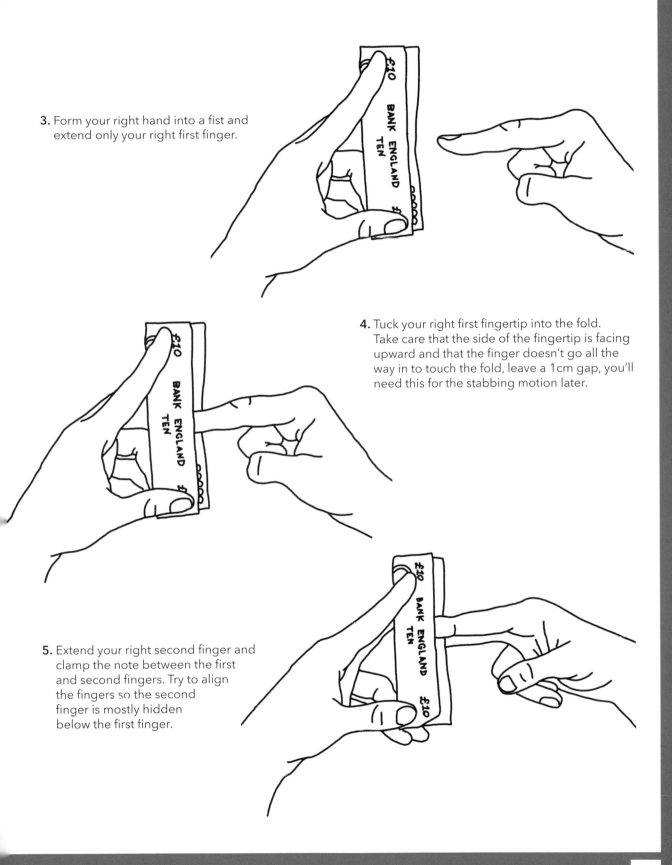

3. Form your right hand into a fist and extend only your right first finger.

4. Tuck your right first fingertip into the fold. Take care that the side of the fingertip is facing upward and that the finger doesn't go all the way in to touch the fold, leave a 1cm gap, you'll need this for the stabbing motion later.

5. Extend your right second finger and clamp the note between the first and second fingers. Try to align the fingers so the second finger is mostly hidden below the first finger.

6. 'I'm going to push my finger right through your banknote,' you say. Then, in a fast motion, slide both your right first and second fingers to the left, as if puncturing the note with your finger. Actually, the first fingertip is positioned against the edge of the fold as the tip of your right second finger is exposed beneath the banknote.

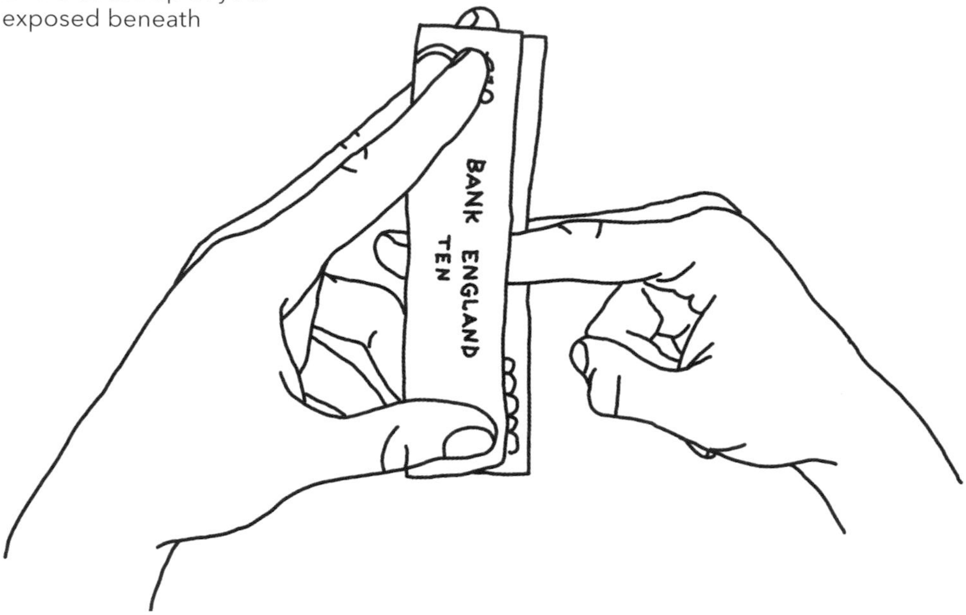

The second illustration shows you the configuration of the banknote and fingers with a see-through note, so you can make sure your positioning is correct. Don't hold this position for more than a couple of seconds or it will become obvious.

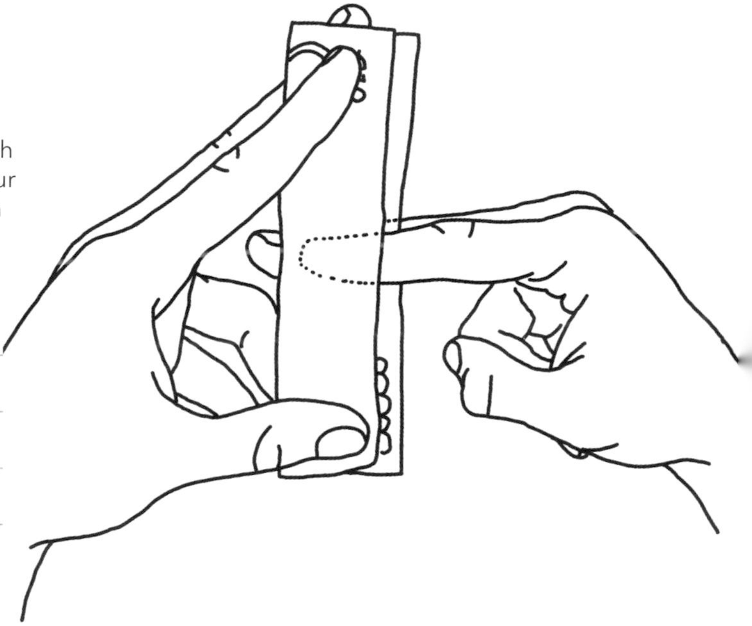

Be aware of your angles when you perform this trick. It looks great from the front, but from the sides or below, it's obvious.

7. 'The only way to get my finger out is to rip through the note.' You apparently rip through the fold of the note, but in this case you are aided by a sound illusion that sounds like tearing. Quickly slide your right hand away from you, holding the note in place with your left thumb and fingers. As you slide the note rapidly between your right first and second fingers, it will make a fthhhhhhhhh sound, like it's tearing against your fingertip. As your right hand clears the banknote, quickly curl in your second finger, leaving just your first finger extended. The spectators won't notice you curl your second finger if you keep the right hand in fast motion as you apparently tear the note in an outward motion.

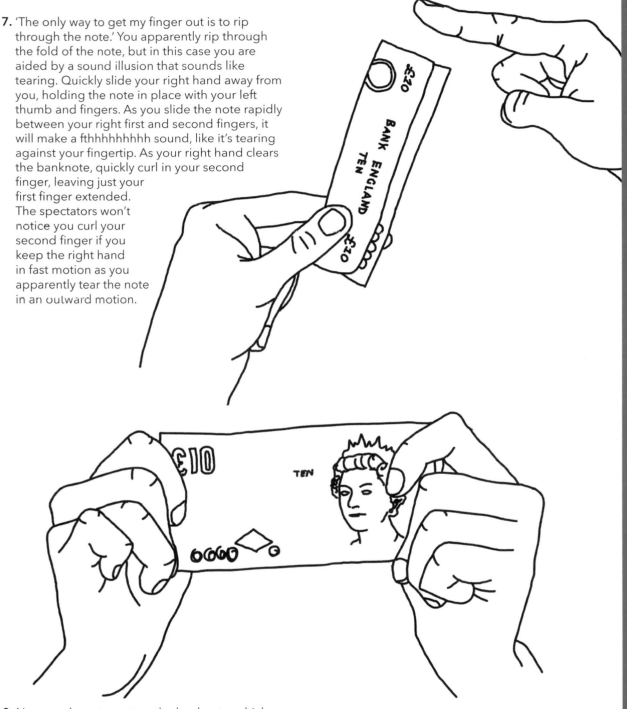

8. Now you have to restore the banknote, which is easy since you never actually tore it. Stare intently at the note, as if healing it with your mind, and then dramatically unfold it to reveal that there are no tears or holes. If you borrowed it, give it back to the spectator. If they're really impressed, maybe they'll give it to you as a tip.

WITH THANKS TO: Japan's Hiro Sakai is the inventor of this quick but effective effect, and I'm grateful that he has granted me permission to teach it to you.

PERFECT PRACTICE MAKES PERFECT

Just because these pieces are easy to learn does not make them easy to do. Even easy magic requires practice. When you practise these pieces, rehearse with discipline and focus. If the TV is on or you're checking your phone every five minutes, your magic may turn out sloppy. But if you practise as if you're in front of your audience, speaking the script of the effect as you do the moves, you'll find that you improve the fluidity of your magic.

I encourage you to find a practice buddy. This is someone you can alternate performing and watching magic with, and also someone who can be honest with you about how to improve. I love the Thomas Edison quote on failure and often keep it in mind when I'm practising: 'I have not failed. I've just found 10,000 ways that won't work.'

But you can only practise an effect so many times in your bedroom. Eventually, you have to try it on some real people!

RINGMASTER

EFFECT
You thread a borrowed rubber band through a borrowed ring and cause the ring to move, on its own, from one end of the rubber band to the other.

When I can, I try to borrow props from spectators. Everyone's first reaction to magic is that the props are gimmicked. This is immediately dispelled if I borrow objects from the audience. This was always a favourite effect to perform because the angles are perfect, there is no secret set-up and it looks incredible.

OVERVIEW
The elasticity of the rubber band is the secret here. Although it appears as if you don't move it at all, you are slowly releasing tension on the rubber band, which gives the perfect illusion of the ring moving on its own.

NEEDED
– Any borrowed ring
– A standard rubber band (regular-thickness rubber bands work best, not the wide and flat ones. You do not want to use one that is too thick)

SET-UP
1. Break the rubber band and thread the ring on it. Hold it at waist height just before you begin to perform. You don't have to hide this action, but you also don't want the performance to begin just yet.

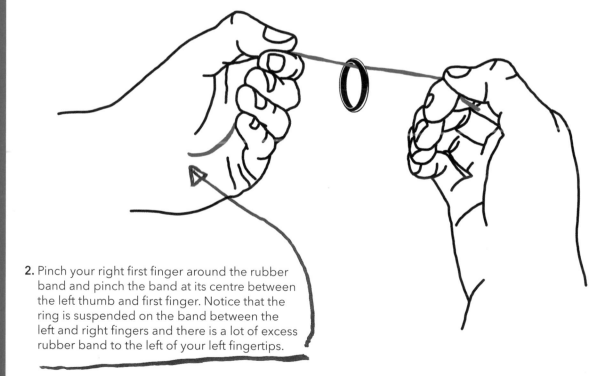

2. Pinch your right first finger around the rubber band and pinch the band at its centre between the left thumb and first finger. Notice that the ring is suspended on the band between the left and right fingers and there is a lot of excess rubber band to the left of your left fingertips.

PERFORMANCE

1. Make a fist with both hands as you raise everything to chest height. Hold your hands about six inches apart, and position the right hand slightly above the left hand. Position the ring so that it is just next to your left first finger and thumb.

Notice that the excess band is concealed in your left fist. It appears, to the audience, as if you merely hold the ring suspended on the rubber band.

2. 'Watch carefully that I hold completely still. It's only your ring that moves.' With your left thumb and first finger, slowly ease your grip on the top strand of the band. Make sure you hold your hands still as you do this.

The ring will begin to move to the right and uphill, as if moving of its own volition. This is a wonderful illusion if performed slowly, so ease your grip very, very slightly.

Because this illusion happens right in front of your face, it's important that you react with enthusiasm. Your reaction will help dictate how the spectators react.

This is nearly always true in magic: you have to believe in what you're doing, as if it's real, for it to feel real to your audience.

3. Continue to ease your grip on the top strand until all the excess band concealed in your left hand is exhausted. Pause for a beat, and then immediately hand the band and the ring back out to a participant. They can examine everything.

WITH THANKS TO: Martin Gardner created this fantastic impromptu magic miracle.

AD ALIVE

EFFECT

You display an array of folded adverts torn out of magazines. On one of them is a picture of a hand holding coins. You fold up this advert, and when you reopen it, the coins have become real… and the hand in the picture is now empty!

The strange thing about magic is that it defies the logic of the world, yet the effects we perform must have an inherent logic. In 'Ad Alive', we know it's not actually possible to make coins in a picture become real. But if we do an effect where coins materialise out of a picture, the effect only works if afterward the picture is also shown to have no more coins in it. In our world, we can do the impossible, but only if it's logical.

OVERVIEW

This is an update on a classic of magic called the 'Buddha Papers'. You display folded papers, each one folded into the next, and change the appearance of the innermost piece of paper. To do this, you will make a secret gimmick by using two identical ads, provided in this book, and glue them back to back. You hide the coins in the folds of the second, secret ad page. The ads look real, but actually contain all the secrets you need to perform 'Ad Alive.'

NEEDED

- An ad torn from a newspaper (this can be anything: a car advert, TV show promotion, ad for pet food – the more bizarre, the better)
- The four tear-out adverts on the following pages
- Coins: two 5p coins, one 10p coin and one 50p coin
- A glue stick

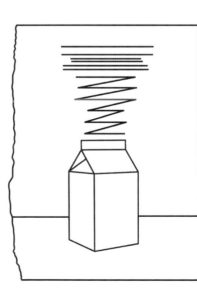

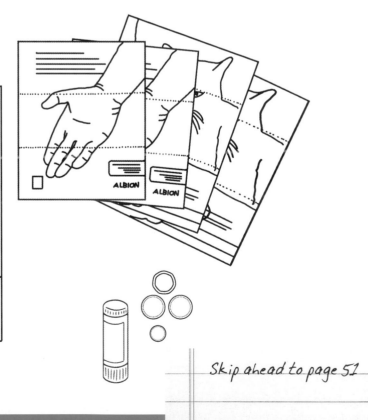

Skip ahead to page 51

ALBIONBANK

THE FUTURE IS YOU

TRIM AWAY THIS SECTION

ABC SAVINGS ISA
Look after the pennies and
the pounds will take
care of themselves.

WINNER

SAVING DOESN'T HAVE
TO BE DIFFICULT. OUR NEW ISA
IS DESIGNED TO GIVE YOU A HELPING
HAND TOWARDS YOUR GOALS.

TRIM AWAY THIS SECTION

There was no way to do it other than the way he said. All the other trainers were busy at the time, so we were not able to say if we would or not. It's very hard to restrain a man with an idea who does not want to be in the area like that. Think about that a bit, and see how far it goes in the back of your mind. He will say that the idea retrains the mind more than class does. Now that I think about it, the real strainer is in the head, and not in the class. Once you get to know the terrains, the rest is easy, so easy that one might think it is right, and not the rest.

There was never a time when we did not go to see new terrains. The usual group of trainers tried to tell us to go. They did not want us to sit lazy and act like we were poor. They

said to find out about the sun spots. They never tried to restrain us from going, but it never works out that way. They put the rule up there, not as a strainer, but more as a way to make us think about if we were doing the right thing or not. It was not put up there as a way that retrains us, but more as a thing that can cause us to not walk away.

I will ever see in my mind the time we went to the space store. The way was not as long as I hoped, and the new terrains along the way were easy. No one who was there tried to restrain us. We were free to go where there was room, and our

trainers said to feel at ease and to feel at home. We told them that the solar array was even nicer than we had hoped. "This is the time that retrains you into the folks that they will want you to be!" We like to think that this is true. Why put a strainer on life when it can be so easy for us?

I will ever see in my mind the time we went to the space store. The way was not as long as I hoped, and the new terrains along the way were easy. There was never a time when we did not go to see new terrains.

There was no way to do it other than the way he said. All the other trainers were busy at the time, so we were not able to say if we would or not. It's very hard to restrain a man with an idea who does not want to be in the area like that. Think about that a bit, and see how far it goes in the back of your mind. He will say that the idea retrains the mind more than class does. Now that I think about it, the real strainer is in the head, and not in the class. Once you get to know the terrains, the rest is easy, so easy that one might think it is right, and not the rest.

This is one of my very favorite card effects because it works over the phone! Despite allowing a participant to use any shuffled deck, you are able to find her selected card...even if you're a thousand miles away!

To perform the trick, just call up a friend and ask her to retrieve a deck of cards. Invite her to shuffle it, and then ask her to cut the deck into four roughly even face-down piles. "The piles don't have to be perfectly even, but you can switch some cards around to even them if you like."

"Now pick up any pile," you say, "and shuffle it again, just to be sure. Now look at the top card. Remember it. Got it? Okay, I'm going to share with you the craziest shuffle I know. It's called the Australian Shuffle. I want you to remember the name so you can show it to your friends later, so let's spell it together to reinforce what it's called: The Australian Shuffle. Spell it with me, transferring one card for each letter from top to bottom: A-U-S-T-R-A-L-I-A-N-S-H-U-F-F-L-E."

Allow the participant to transfer cards for each letter, until she has spelled "Australian Shuffle." Now say, "This shuffle comes from Australia, which is the land down under. That's why we mix cards down, and then under. Take the top card and deal it down on the table. Take the next card, and deal it under the packet. Continue like that until you've dealt through all the cards, with just one left in your hand."

Give your participant a few moments to complete the Australian Shuffle. Ask her which card she selected, and then invite her to turn over the card left in her hand...her reaction, even over the phone, should be intense.

This works as long as the participant divides the piles roughly evenly. If there are less than eight or more than sixteen cards, the trick won't work, so make sure to encourage the participant to "even the piles out" after she cuts.

CREDITS: This effect was created by British magic legend Alex Elmsley, who I had the pleasure of meeting when I was a kid.

THE FUTURE IS YOU

TRIM AWAY THIS SECTION

ABC SAVINGS ISA
Look after the pennies and the pounds will take care of themselves.

WINNER

SAVING DOESN'T HAVE TO BE DIFFICULT. OUR NEW ISA IS DESIGNED TO GIVE YOU A HELPING HAND TOWARDS YOUR GOALS.

TRIM AWAY THIS SECTION

There was no way to do it other than the way he said. All the other trainers were busy at the time, so we were not able to say if we would or not. It's very hard to restrain a man with an idea who does not want to be in the area like that. Think about that a bit, and see how far it goes in the back of your mind. He will say that the idea retrains the mind more than class does. Now that I think about it, the real strainer is in the head, and not in the class. Once you get to know the terrains, the rest is easy, so easy that one might think it is right, and not the rest.

There was never a time when we did not go to see new terrains. The usual group of trainers tried to tell us to go. They did not want us to sit lazy and act like we were poor. They

said to find out about the sun spots. They never tried to restrain us from going, but it never works out that way. They put the rule up there, not as a strainer, but more as a way to make us think about if we were doing the right thing or not. It was not put up there as a way that retrains us, but more as a thing that can cause us to not walk away.

I will ever see in my mind the time we went to the space store. The way was not as long as I hoped, and the new terrains along the way were easy. No one who was there tried to restrain us. We were free to go where there was room, and our

trainers said to feel at ease and to feel at home. We told them that the solar array was even nicer than we had hoped. "This is the time that retrains you into the folks that they will want you to be!" We like to think that this is true. Why put a strainer on life when it can be so easy for us?

I will ever see in my mind the time we went to the space store. The way was not as long as I hoped, and the new terrains along the way were easy. There was never a time when we did not go to see new terrains.

There was no way to do it other than the way he said. All the other trainers were busy at the time, so we were not able to say if we would or not. It's very hard to restrain a man with an idea who does not want to be in the area like that. Think about that a bit, and see how far it goes in the back of your mind. He will say that the idea retrains the mind more than class does. Now that I think about it, the real strainer is in the head, and not in the class. Once you get to know the terrains, the rest is easy, so easy that one might think it is right, and not the rest.

This is one of my very favorite card effects because it works over the phone! Despite allowing a participant to use any shuffled deck, you are able to find her selected card...even if you're a thousand miles away!

To perform the trick, just call up a friend and ask her to retrieve a deck of cards. Invite her to shuffle it, and then ask her to cut the deck into four roughly even face-down piles. "The piles don't have to be perfectly even, but you can switch some cards around to even them if you like."

"Now pick up any pile," you say, "and shuffle it again, just to be sure. Now look at the top card. Remember it. Got it? Okay, I'm going to share with you the craziest shuffle I know. It's called the Australian Shuffle. I want you to remember the name so you can show it to your friends later, so let's spell it together to reinforce what it's called: The Australian Shuffle. Spell it with me, transferring one card for each letter from top to bottom: A-U-S-T-R-A-L-I-A-N-S-H-U-F-F-L-E."

Allow the participant to transfer cards for each letter, until she has spelled "Australian Shuffle." Now say, "This shuffle comes from Australia, which is the land down under. That's why we mix cards down, and then under. Take the top card and deal it down on the table. Take the next card, and deal it under the packet. Continue like that until you've dealt through all the cards, with just one left in your hand."

Give your participant a few moments to complete the Australian Shuffle. Ask her which card she selected, and then invite her to turn over the card left in her hand...her reaction, even over the phone, should be intense.

This works as long as the participant divides the piles roughly evenly. If there are less than eight or more than sixteen cards, the trick won't work, so make sure to encourage the participant to "even the piles out" after she cuts.

CREDITS: This effect was created by British magic legend Alex Elmsley, who I had the pleasure of meeting when I was a kid.

AVAILABLE NOW

 **Approved** By the DVAA

 **Omega 3** For a healthy heart

☺ **YUM!** Because...just because

not all cats are equal
your cat deserves the best

purfect
ready for a feast?

There was no way to do it other than the way he said. All the other trainers were busy at the time, so we were not able to say if we would or not. It's very hard to restrain a man with an idea who does not want to be in the area like that. Think about that a bit, and see how far it goes in the back of your mind. He will say that the idea retrains the mind more than class does. Now that I think about it, the real strainer is in the head, and not in the class. Once you get to know the terrains, the rest is easy, so easy that one might think it is right, and not the rest.

There was never a time when we did not go to see new terrains. The usual group of trainers tried to tell us to go. They did not want us to sit lazy and act like we were poor. They said to find out about the sun spots. They never tried to restrain us from going, but it never works out that way. They put the rule up there, not as a strainer, but more as a way to make us think about if we

GLUE

HERE

were doing the right thing or not. It was not put up there as a way that retrains us, but more as a thing that can cause us to not walk away.

I will ever see in my mind the time we went to the space store. The way was not as long as I hoped, and the new terrains along the way were easy. No one who was there tried to restrain us. We were free to go where there was room, and our trainers said to feel at ease and to feel at home. We told them that the solar array was even nicer than we had hoped. "This is the time that retrains you into the folks that they will want you to be!" We like to think that this is true. Why put a strainer on life when it can be so easy for us?

The black hole gave us new hope for us to go to and visit all the new terrains. Was there ever to be more of a strainer than the one that this one had given us? We hoped like crazy and all that our trainers would be able to tell us all that we asked and tried to know. "Don't ever try to restrain any of your great ideas in your quest for the truth about the black holes that you may and will find," our trainers would tell us. v

This is one of my very favorite card effects because it works over the phone! Despite allowing a participant to use any shuffled deck, you are able to find her selected card...even if you're a thousand miles away!

> The black hole gave us new hope to go to and visit all the new terrains. They never tried to restain us. They always encouraged us!
> **– Davis Williams**

To perform the trick, just call up a friend and ask her to retrieve a deck of cards. Invite her to shuffle it, and then ask her to cut the deck into four roughly even face-down piles. "The piles don't have to be perfectly even, but you can switch some cards around to even them if you like."

"Now pick up any pile," you say, "and shuffle it again, just to be sure. Now look at the top card. Remember it. Got it? Okay, I'm going to share with you the craziest shuffle I know. It's called the Australian Shuffle. I want you to remember the name so you can show it to your friends later, so let's spell it together to reinforce what it's called: The Australian Shuffle. Spell it with me, transferring one card for each letter from top to b o t t o m : A-U-S-T-R-A-L-I-A-N-S-H-U-F-F-L-E."

Allow the participant to transfer cards for each letter, until she has spelled "Australian Shuffle." Now say, "This shuffle comes from Australia, which is the land down under. That's why we mix cards down, and then under. Take the top card and deal it down on the table. Take the next card, and deal it under the packet. Continue like that until you've dealt through all the cards, with just one left in your hand."

Give your participant a few moments to complete the Australian Shuffle. Ask her which card she selected, and then invite her to turn over the card left in her hand...her reaction, even over the phone, should be intense.

This works as long as the participant divides the piles roughly evenly. If there are less than eight or more than sixteen cards, the trick won't work, so make sure to encourage the participant to "even the piles out" after she cuts.

CREDITS: This effect was created by British magic legend Alex Elmsley, who I had the pleasure of meeting when I was a kid.

AVAILABLE NOW

✓ **Approved**
By the DVAA

♥ **Omega 3**
For a healthy heart

☺ **YUM!**
Because...just because

not all cats are equal
your cat deserves the best

purfect
ready for a feast?

There was no way to do it other than the way he said. All the other trainers were busy at the time, so we were not able to say if we would or not. It's very hard to restrain a man with an idea who does not want to be in the area like that. Think about that a bit, and see how far it goes in the back of your mind. He will say that the idea retrains the mind more than class does. Now that I think about it, the real strainer is in the head, and not in the class. Once you get to know the terrains, the rest is easy, so easy that one might think it is right, and not the rest.

There was never a time when we did not go to see new terrains. The usual group of trainers tried to tell us to go. They did not want us to sit lazy and act like we were poor. They said to find out about the sun spots. They never tried to restrain us from going, but it never works out that way. They put the rule up there, not as a strainer, but more as a way to make us think about if we

GLUE

HERE

were doing the right thing or not. It was not put up there as a way that retrains us, but more as a thing that can cause us to not walk away.

I will ever see in my mind the time we went to the space store. The way was not as long as I hoped, and the new terrains along the way were easy. No one who was there tried to restrain us. We were free to go where there was room, and our trainers said to feel at ease and to feel at home. We told them that the solar array was even nicer than we had hoped. "This is the time that retrains you into the folks that they will want you to be!" We like to think that this is true. Why put a strainer on life when it can be so easy for us?

The black hole gave us new hope for us to go to and visit all the new terrains. Was there ever to be more of a strainer than the one that this one had given us? We hoped like crazy and all that our trainers would be able to tell us all that we asked and tried to know. "Don't ever try to restrain any of your great ideas in your quest for the truth about the black holes that you may and will find," our trainers would tell us. v

This is one of my very favorite card effects because it works over the phone! Despite allowing a participant to use any shuffled deck, you are able to find her selected card...even if you're a thousand miles away!

To perform the trick, just call up a friend and ask her to retrieve a deck of cards. Invite her to shuffle it, and then ask her to cut the deck into four roughly even face-down piles. "The piles don't have to be perfectly even, but you can switch some cards around to even them if you like."

"Now pick up any pile," you say, "and shuffle it again, just to be sure. Now look at the top card. Remember it. Got it? Okay, I'm going to share with you the craziest shuffle I know. It's called the Australian Shuffle. I want you to remember the name so you can show it to your friends later, so let's spell it together to reinforce what it's called: The Australian Shuffle. Spell it with me, transferring one card for each letter from top to b o t t o m : A-U-S-T-R-A-L-I-A-N-S-H-U-F-F-L-E."

Allow the participant to transfer cards for each letter, until she has spelled "Australian Shuffle." Now say, "This shuffle comes from Australia, which is the land down under. That's why we mix cards down, and then under. Take the top card and deal it down on the table. Take the next card, and deal it under the packet. Continue like that until you've dealt through all the cards, with just one left in your hand."

Give your participant a few moments to complete the Australian Shuffle. Ask her which card she selected, and then invite her to turn over the card left in her hand...her reaction, even over the phone, should be intense.

This works as long as the participant divides the piles roughly evenly. If there are less than eight or more than sixteen cards, the trick won't work, so make sure to encourage the participant to "even the piles out" after she cuts.

CREDITS: This effect was created by British magic legend Alex Elmsley, who I had the pleasure of meeting when I was a kid.

> The black hole gave us new hope to go to and visit all the new terrains. They never tried to restain us. They always encouraged us!
> – **Davis Williams**

SET-UP

1. You need to select one ad yourself from a newspaper of your choice. It can be anything you like, but it's important that this page is larger than the cat food adverts contained in this book.

2. Now tear out the two ads for cat food on the previous pages. Notice that this ad is larger than the two sheets that advertise Albion Bank. It's okay if the edges where you tear are rough. In fact, it's better if the cat food adverts look like you ripped them from a magazine at random. Notice that the back of each one contains boring columns of text.

3. Next tear out both pages advertising Albion Bank. Cut away the excess grey boxes next to and above the ad, so both of the Albion Bank pages are smaller than the cat food adverts.

4. You must now fold the cat food pages separately. Each one is folded in the exact same way, and there are secret dotted lines built into the design that you can use as a guide.

5. On the first cat advert, fold the bottom of the page upward along the red line.

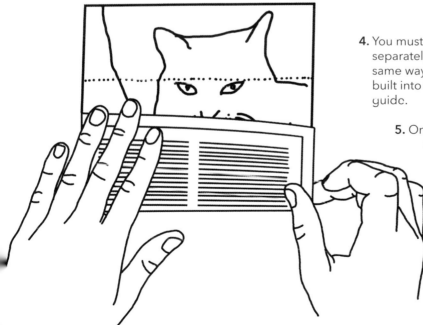

6. Now fold the top down along the green line.

7. Fold the left side along the yellow line.

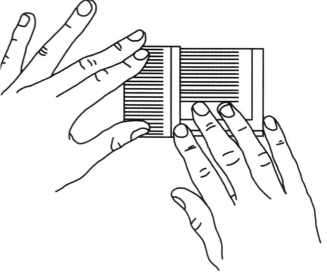

8. Fold the right side along the blue line.

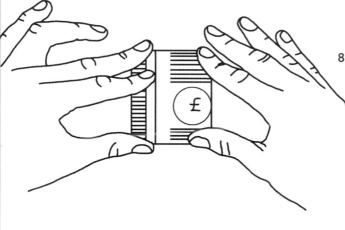

9. Now repeat this fold with the second cat food advert. When completed, you'll have two identical folded pages.

GLUE
HERE

10. Using a glue stick, stick the two cat food pages together, back to back. To make it easy I have added text to these sections that says GLUE HERE. You now have a gimmick that has two identical cat food ads on the inside of each folded page.

There is one important detail to note. When both sides of the gimmick are folded, there is a black circle uppermost on each side. One side is just a black circle, and one side has a £ symbol on it. This symbol is the only way to tell which side is up.

11. Fold the two Albion Bank ads in the same way you folded the cat food pages. The coloured guideline folds will help you as you go.

12. The only difference between the bank ads is that one shows an empty hand and the other one shows a hand with four coins. Open the ad with the empty hand and carefully place the four coins into the centre section. Refold this page back into a small packet.

Notice that when it's folded up, this Albion Bank page also has a black circle with a £ sign on it. This will help you remember which page goes where and which side of the packets the real money is.

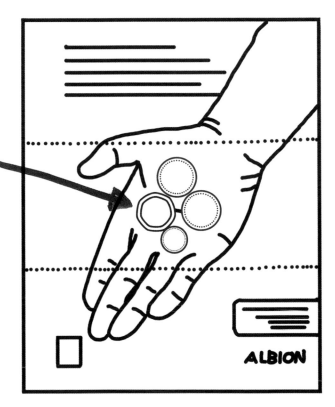

ALBION

13. Open the cat food page gimmick, on the side with £ logo showing, and place the bank page/packet (with the real coins folded inside) into the cat page gimmick and fold it up.

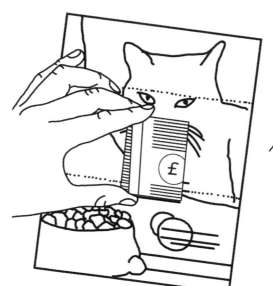

14. Fold the other Albion Bank ad back together: the bottom up, the top down, left to right and right to left. Place this page inside the other side of the gimmick. Notice that both this bank ad and the cat food ad on this side have a solid black circle on the outside. This helps you remember that circle goes with circle, £ goes with £.

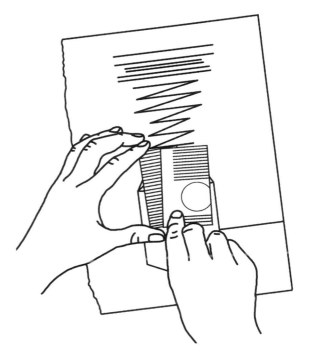

15. Fold the larger, newspaper ad in the same way you folded the other pages. Make sure that you leave enough room to place the 'nested bundle of pages' aka our double-sided gimmick, inside it.

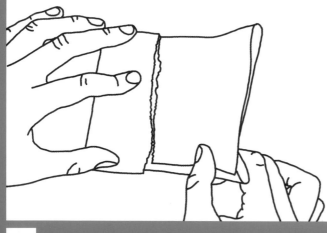

16. You're now ready to perform! I realise that is a lot of preparation, but the great news is that you're done for ever. Now the effect is a breeze to perform, and easy to reset.

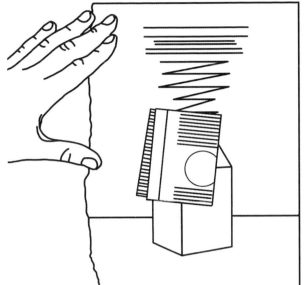

1. 'I like to do magic with things I see, so sometimes I save ads… like these.' Take out the bundle and unfold the newspaper ad. Show it to the audience for a moment, and then place it on the table.

2. 'Or this one is for cat food. I haven't thought of a good effect for this one yet.' Unfold the cat food ad. Before you unfold it, double-check that the black circle with nothing inside it is facing up. You don't want to expose the coins - your big ending - before the time is right.

Show the cat food advert but don't turn it over or you'll expose the gimmick. Just place this ad on top of the unfolded newspaper ad on the table as you remove the last folded paper.

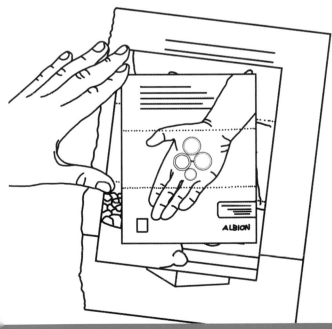

3. Unfold the bank advert. 'When I saw this, I knew immediately what I wanted to do with it. It's an ad for a bank, about making money. I'll show you how I make money.' Hand a participant this ad and have them examine it front and back. Ask them to remember the coins in the hand.

4. Fold up the paper in the usual way and place it inside the cat advert. Fold up the cat advert, but as you place it inside the newspaper, turn it over. Now the £ sign should be facing upward.

5. Fold the newspaper around the paper bundle. 'All I do is tap the paper like this. And illusion becomes reality!' Unfold the newspaper and remove the gimmick. Unfold the cat advert, again taking care not to turn it over. Carefully remove the other bank ad. NB You have to treat this paper gently or the coins will clink against each other prematurely.

6. Slowly unfold this bank advert to show that the coins in the hand are now real coins. Dump them into the participant's hands and then point out that the hand in the picture is now empty!

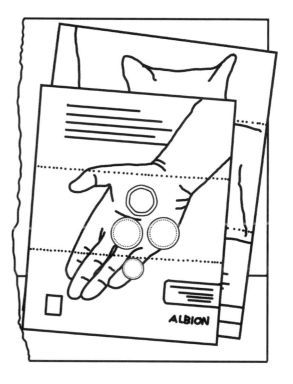

WITH THANKS TO: This effect has been known as the 'Buddha Papers' since the 1930s, but it actually goes back to the Middle Ages! It was used to swindle people out of their coins. A hustler would ask to borrow a coin and wrap it in layers of cloth or paper... and when the paper was unfolded again, the coin was gone!

THE POWER OF MYSTERY: BANKSY

I've always been a big fan of graffiti. It reminds me of when I would sit on the train down to London and look out of the window, fascinated by the trackside graffiti. It would continually change to reflect the artist's thoughts at the current time.

Banksy's work fascinated me because, like a great magician, he had a secret. His secret was his real identity, and like the best magicians, he still hasn't revealed it! If you watch *Magician Impossible* you'll know that we create the feeling that you never know where I'll appear or what I'll do next. This was inspired by Banksy's approach and goes against the magician's tradition of pre-promoting their every appearance.

FREEZE

EFFECT
With a simple tap of your finger, you cause a water bottle to visibly freeze. Optional: The spectators can immediately examine the solid, frozen bottle of ice.

The author Arthur C. Clarke famously wrote, 'Any sufficiently advanced technology is indistinguishable from magic.' He was right – if you use science that your audience doesn't understand, it looks like magic. And that's exactly what 'Freeze' is about.

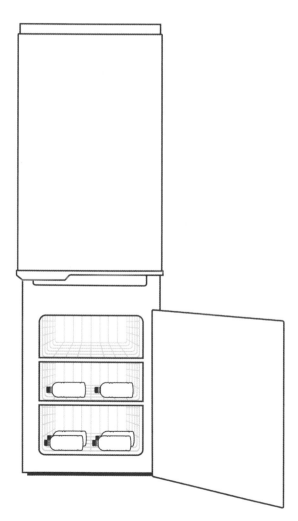

OVERVIEW
The water bottle is already freezing cold, but not yet frozen. A simple tap, believe it or not, will cause the water to turn to ice right before your eyes.

NEEDED
– Five or six bottles of still mineral water
  (NB You can't use tap water)
– A freezer

SET-UP
1. 'Freeze' will take some experimentation since every freezer is different. Place five or six bottles of water inside your freezer, evenly spaced from each other, lying on their sides.

2. In my freezer the temperature can be set exactly, and I set it to -24 °C. In other freezers, the temperature may be on a scale from 1 to 10, in which case you should start at 5 or 6 and adjust later depending on the conditions.

   You will need to establish precisely how long it takes for the bottles to freeze. To do this, let the bottles sit for 90 minutes, and then quickly open the freezer drawer to see if any of them have started to freeze. You'll see small, floating ice crystals at first; this is a sign the bottle is ready. If you don't observe any ice crystals after 90 minutes, check back every ten minutes until they begin to appear.

3. Note the total time it takes for this bottle and brand of water to form ice crystals. Mine took 2 hours and 35 minutes. Subtract 15 minutes from this total and note this time. In our example, 2 hours and 20 minutes is the magic number. You don't have to time the effect to the minute, but you have about a 15-minute window after 2 hours and 20 minutes (or whatever time you calculate) to make the magic work.

4. You'll have to time this effect exactly for best results, or simply perform it at your house for friends at exactly the right moment. When the bottles are ready to perform, carefully remove the bottle, keeping it horizontal.

PERFORMANCE
1. To understand how the effect works, I'll briefly explain the science behind it. The water inside the bottles is actually below freezing temperature, but it hasn't frozen through because there are no impurities for the crystals to build upon. A firm tap on the side of the bottle creates the necessary impurities for the crystals to instantly connect, from bottom to top. So be careful as you handle the water bottle because even an accidental tap may be enough to prematurely freeze the contents.

2. Display the water bottle to the audience and wipe off any condensation forming on the outside. You want the clear plastic to be clean enough to see through before you perform your magic.

3. Offer to change the water into ice, and form your right hand into a fist. Give the side of the bottle a firm tap, as if you're gently punching its side; aim for the label.

4. That's it! Let science work its own magic, and you'll see the water freeze over from bottom to top, turning into solid ice. You can immediately hand out the bottle for examination because the water really is frozen through.

COINCEALED

EFFECT
You remove several objects from your pocket (a coin, a pen, a watch and nail clippers) and ask a participant to think of any one. You reveal that the objects themselves spell out the chosen item.

I love effects where the participant believes you have psychologically influenced their choices. This effect, created by mentalist Raj Madhok, is something you can do at any time, with no preparation, once you know the secret.

OVERVIEW
Once you have borrowed or displayed the four objects mentioned above, you will apparently give the participant a free choice to eliminate three of the objects, thus selecting one. To do this, you show them a simple game. But this 'game' is actually a magician's tool called a force. In particular, this is the PATEO force, developed by Roy Baker. Despite the casual appearance, the participant will always choose the coin.

NEEDED
You need nothing in advance, but must be able to borrow:
- A watch
- Nail clippers (the kind that have three riveted pieces that can form an 'N' shape)
- Any coin
- Any pen or pencil

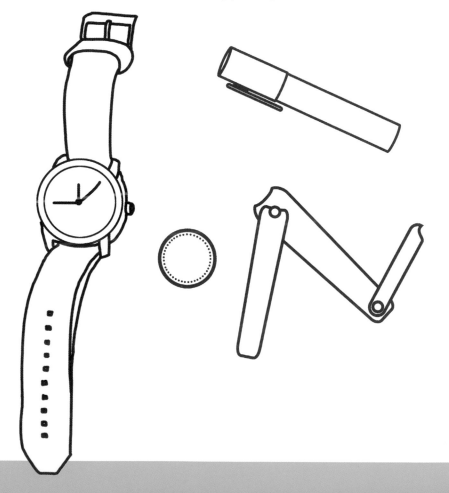

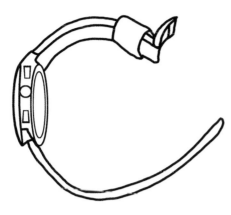

PERFORMANCE

1. Borrow any watch that has a traditional leather band. When turned on its side, the watch must be able to make a 'C' shape. Orient this 'C' so that it is legible for the spectators facing you.

2. Borrow or provide any coin and pen, and place them next to the watch 'C' so that you begin to spell 'COIN' with the objects: C, O, I. Again, take care that the letters are oriented properly for the audience, upside-down to you.

3. It may be difficult or awkward to borrow nail clippers, so this is the one object you may wish to carry with you. As you display the clippers, casually unfold them into an 'N' shape, and place them into the row to complete the word 'COIN.' Of course, don't point out this configuration just yet. That part comes at the end.

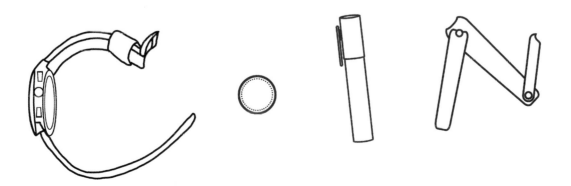

4. 'A simple but fascinating demonstration with four random objects. Do you think it's possible I could influence you to choose one of these, and not another one? Believe it or not, I've already begun to influence you. We're going to play a simple game, you and I, and despite both of us having complete freedom of choice, I believe the decisions you will make have already been decided. You'll see what I mean.'

Now you explain a simple game, which is really a way of forcing the coin. The PATEO force is an acronym for Point-At-Two-Eliminate-One, or P.A.T.E.O. It works like this: the participant points at any two of the objects and you, the magician, eliminate one. Then it's your turn to point at two objects, and they choose to eliminate one. You go back and forth like this three times until only one object remains.

It sounds fair, but there's a catch. You can always determine the forced object as long as you follow three simple rules:

The participant starts. With an even number of objects, it's critical that the participant points to two objects first. If you want to use this wonderful force for other effects, just make sure you use an even number of objects (or if you use an odd number, you start the game).

When it's your turn to point to two objects, do NOT point at the coin! You can't predict which three objects will be left when it's your turn, but it doesn't matter. Point at the two objects that are not the coin, and everything will work out fine.

When it's your turn to eliminate, don't eliminate the coin! Duh.

5. Let's assume you have explained to the participant the premise of the simple game: that you'll alternate pointing to objects and eliminating them. They begin, and they point at the watch and the coin.

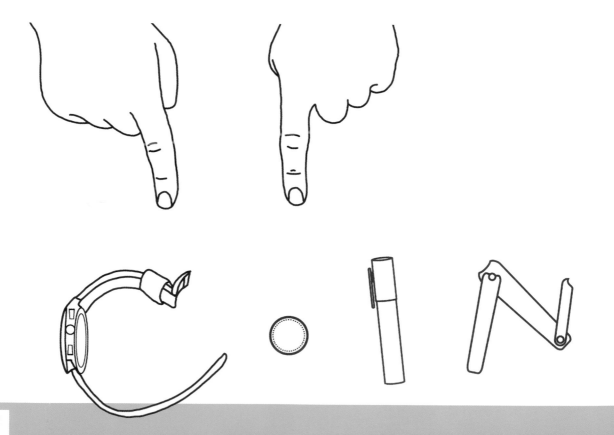

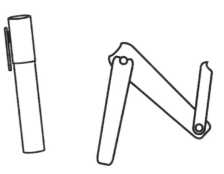

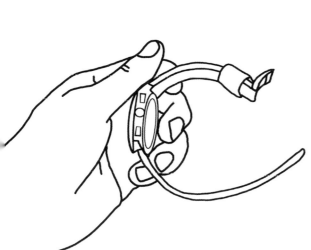

6. 'Okay, you pointed to two objects, so I eliminate one. I'll go with, um, the watch.' Use your best acting abilities to make it appear as if you're deciding on a whim, randomly. Actually, you have to eliminate the watch because you can't eliminate the coin. Slide the watch back, toward yourself, to show that it's eliminated.

7. 'Now it's my turn. I'll point to, well, I guess… these two.' Again, act as if you're pointing at two objects at random, but now you must point to the pen and the clippers (because one of the rules is that you do not point to the coin).

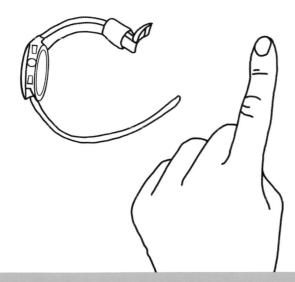

8. Ask the participant to eliminate either one of the objects you're pointing to. Invite them to slide it toward you, eliminating it. Perhaps they eliminate the pen.

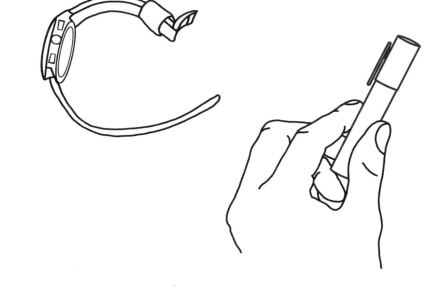

9. Now it's their turn to point to two objects. Eliminate the other object, which in our example will be the clippers. Slide the clippers toward yourself and point out that the coin is the selected object. 'Did you feel like your choices were fair? Remember, you could have easily eliminated the clippers, or chosen the watch, but you ended up choosing the coin. We're often drawn to things we don't understand. Even when the answer is right in front of us.'

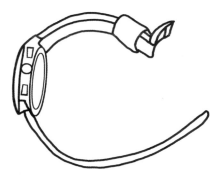

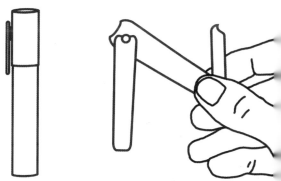

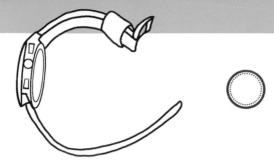

10. Pause for a moment and slide the coin toward yourself, back in line with the other objects. Smile, and pause for a moment. The spectators will stare blankly at you and the objects. 'You chose the coin. C-O-I-N.' Now point to each 'letter' in turn, as you call out again, 'C-O-I N.'

WITH THANKS TO: The PATEO force, as mentioned elsewhere, was created by Roy Baker. Raj Madhok created this trick.

MICHAEL JACKSON: FINDING YOUR OWN STYLE

When I was a kid, MJ was the biggest performer on the planet. Everything about him was magical, from the way he dressed to the way he danced on stage. He produced what I consider to be the greatest music video of all time, 'Smooth Criminal', which includes some incredible magic.

His story also resonated with me. He grew up in a poor neighbourhood in Indiana, and it was his passion and work ethic that catapulted him to become a global icon.

MJ's style was influenced by the likes of James Brown, Fred Astaire and Bob Fosse but ultimately he took these influences and created something that felt wholly original and defined an era in popular culture. As a magician it's critical to find your own style and unique authenticity. How can you take your influences and make them your own? What persona works best with your personality/style of magic?

I was due to meet Michael Jackson during the 'This Is It' tour at the 02 Arena in 2009. He had seen my videos and was apparently a fan of my magic but tragically he passed away unexpectedly, and I never got to meet my hero. In 2016 I became the first magician in history to perform at the O2 arena and although I was super nervous, I told myself I had to get out there and give it my all – MJ style!

FLOATING GUM

EFFECT
Chewing gum floats from out of your mouth, around your head and then right back between your lips!

If this effect sounds unbelievable, then read on! It's not only possible, but easy to perform. You'll have to construct the gimmick yourself, but once this is done, you'll have the ability to perform a miracle that people will never forget.

OVERVIEW
This is based on an old stunt in which, historically, a woman with long hair causes her gum to fly around her head and back into her mouth. The way it works is this: her wad of chewing gum is connected to one strand of her hair. In the short time in which she blows it out of her mouth and swings it around her head, it's impossible to notice the hair, which blends into the background.

I don't have long hair, so I have altered this classic effect so that I can perform it in any environment – as long as I'm wearing a hat.

NEEDED
- A 40cm piece of invisible thread sold in sewing shops (or if you have long hair, you can use one strand of that).
- A wad of gum
- A baseball-style hat

A gimmick is a prop that seems normal but actually is set up to do something secret.

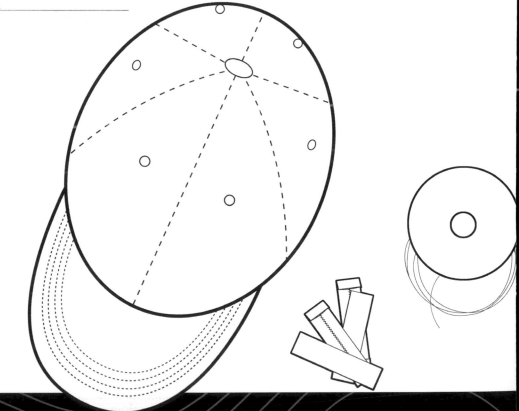

SET-UP

1. Begin by chewing your gum for a moment; you want it moist and sticky for the preparation. Remove the gum from your mouth and fold in one end of the thread. Wrap it through the gum twice so that it's locked into place.

2. Anchor the other end of the thread/hair on the top of your hat by tying the end around the button 'top' piece on the very top of the hat.

Make sure that when the gum hangs off the hat it rests just beside your mouth.

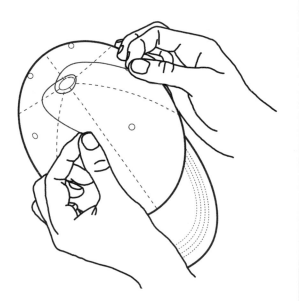

3. When you're ready to perform, pop the hat on your head and carefully run the thread along the left side of the hat's brim, and into your mouth. Chew the gum casually, taking care to avoid the gag reflex from chewing gum with thread or hair in it!

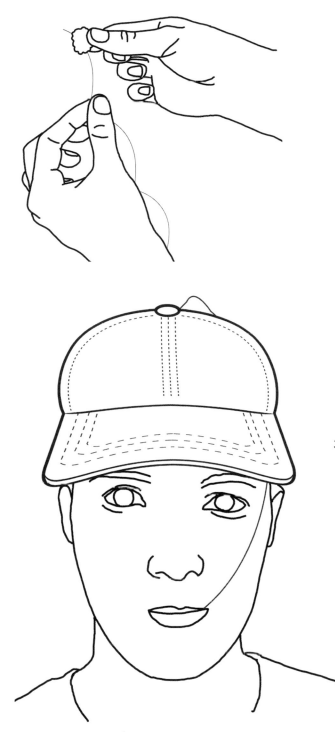

PERFORMANCE

1. When someone asks you to do some magic, offer to show them a quick, amazing effect. 'Watch the gum,' you say, as you push the gum forward, gripping it gently between your teeth and displaying it.

2. With a gentle, quick gust of breath, blow the gum out of your mouth as you gently rock your head to the left in a circular motion. You want the gum to fly out of your mouth and around the back of your head, clearing the material on the hat until it flies back to the right hand side of the brim.

This will take practice. If you blow the gum too hard, you risk breaking the thread or causing the gum to fly erratically. If you don't blow with enough force, you risk standing in front of your friends with a piece of hairy gum dangling by your face. But if you practise, you'll be able to swing it around your head gently in a way that looks truly impossible.

3. Now for the catch: The moment you blow the gum out of your mouth, open your mouth wide in preparation for catching it on its return journey. This is not an exact science, but your success rate improves if you tilt your head back and open your mouth to make the widest target possible.

4. The last step is to act casual after you catch the gum, chewing as you shrug your shoulders. To 'clean up' the effect, take your hat off and as you pass it in front of your face, secretly spit the gum into the hat. Now it's set for next time.

One worry in magic is that people often ask to examine the props after a performance so that they might discover the secret. The good news here is that nobody (well, almost nobody) is going to ask to examine the chewing gum in your mouth!

WITH THANKS TO: This is actually an old gag whose creator is lost to time. Paul Harris, one of the most famous magic creators of our time, pointed out that the gag could be used as a magic effect.

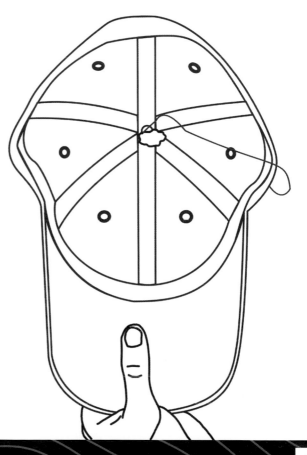

THE FOUR STAGES OF LEARNING

It is said that there are four different stages of learning any new skill. Once you identify where you are at each stage, you'll then be able to learn exactly what you need to do to improve. I often remind myself of these four steps when learning a new piece:

1. **Unconscious incompetence**
   The very start of learning a skill – not realising that you aren't as good as you could be! Everyone goes through this stage, but when you start performing more often you'll quickly move on to the next stage of learning.

2. **Conscious incompetence**
   The more you learn and perform for people, the more you realise that you need more practice! The best magicians rehearse their magic every day and I encourage you to do the same. The more you practise, the better you'll get.

3. **Conscious competence**
   I'm always proud of myself when I reach this stage because it is when the effect starts to get amazing reactions from my audiences! It's when you can perform the effect but still need to focus on making sure you get everything right.

4. **Unconscious competence**
   This is also called 'mastery'. It's where you have practised and performed so much that you can perform the effect automatically while focusing on creating the best experience for your audience. This takes hundreds of performances, but it's worthwhile.

   I'm sharing these four points because I want you to understand that while magic isn't always easy, it is extremely rewarding if you put the work in.

PEN THROUGH COIN

EFFECT

A glass bottle, a pen and a coin are displayed. The coin is balanced on top of the opening of the bottle so that it entirely covers the opening. You then cause a pen to pass through the coin, landing inside the bottle. Immediately after you perform the effect, everything is examinable.

I used to work on all my new material in pubs, and my favourite type of magic is exactly this sort: effects with borrowed objects.

NEEDED

Everything can be borrowed, but you will need:
- A banknote
- A coin (a 2p coin works well)
- An empty bottle
- A pen (the heavier the better; cheap plastic pens do not work as well)

The coin needs to fit over the opening of the bottle without falling through.

PERFORMANCE

1. There is no preparation, so you can assemble the props required right in front of the audience. Place the bottle on the table and balance the coin on top, resting across the opening. Point out that with the coin in place, nothing can pass in or out of the bottle.

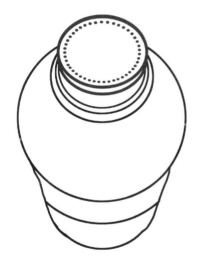

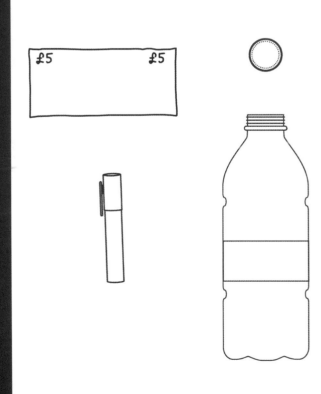

2. Roll the banknote into a tube and place it over the neck of the bottle, covering the coin from the spectators' view. If the banknote is new, it will hold its tubular shape on its own. If not, you may have to hold it in position to stop it from prematurely unravelling.

3. 'You've seen those amazing bottles with model ships inside. They're like magic; how did the ship get into the bottle? I don't have a ship here, but I'll do something equally impossible. I'll put this pen into this bottle, through this coin.' Invite the participant to peer above the note, into the bottle, to verify the coin is still blocking the opening. Then have all the spectators stand back.

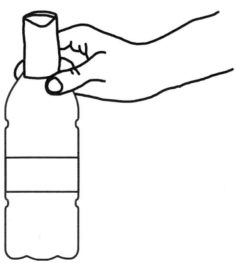

4. With your right hand, hold one end of the pen just above the top edge of the banknote tube. Release the pen so it falls straight down into the tube, striking the coin. The weight of the pen will secretly cause the coin to flip on its side for a moment, allowing the pen to pass through. Immediately and automatically, the coin will fall back into position.

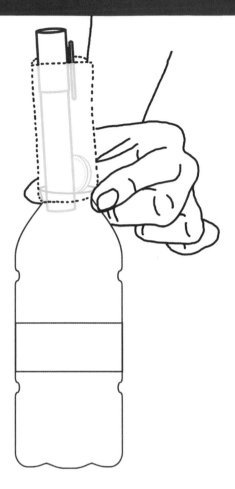

5. Carefully remove the banknote tube so you don't disrupt the coin balanced on the edge of the bottle's opening. The illusion of the pen penetrating the coin, into the bottle, is perfect.

WITH THANKS TO: This is an old effect that was originally sold by U.F. Grant. The great Paul Harris, along with Don Tanner, modernised the effect by using a pen and banknote.

PAUL HARRIS

The creator of this piece, Paul Harris, is one of the greatest magicians, yet he never performs shows. How can this be? Because Paul decided long ago that his interest was in creating magic illusions.

Paul was among the first to look at a deck of cards not only as a gambling tool, but as 52 pieces of paper. He created magic in which you fold, burn, tear and write on playing cards. This style of magic is weird, but also unforgettable. Growing up, I did lots of Paul Harris effects, and I'm honoured that Paul has allowed me to teach one of his pieces to you.

POSTCARD POWER

EFFECT

Twenty postcards are displayed and one is freely chosen. The backs are then all shown to be blank except for the chosen one, which is inscribed with a personal message to the participant, including their name.

The best magic is personal. In terms of magic methods, this is a very simple piece. It uses what magicians call a 'force' to influence the participant to choose the postcard I want them to choose. But that's not the point. The effect is that there is a personal message to the person who chose the postcard, and this can affect the participant on a personal and emotional level as it will be unique to each person you perform it to. When I used to perform this effect, I had several participants tell me, years later, that they saved the postcard I gave them.

OVERVIEW

You determine in advance who you will use to perform 'Postcard Power', and you write them a personal note on the back of a postcard. You use a force to ensure the participant selects the only postcard with a message on it.

NEEDED

- Twenty postcards. They can be from anywhere, but a variety of places and climates is nice. You can find these postcards as you travel or simply order a packet online. You can also download pre-made ones, ready to print out, from **dynamomagician.com/secrets**
- A pen

SET-UP

The only preparation is to write a personal message on the back of one of the postcards. If you know they are going on holiday soon or have a dream holiday destination, use that place! For example:

Dear Rachel,
Have a great time in Vegas!
Love, Dynamo

1. The point here is to make the message personal. If you know the participant well, this is easier. You can relate the message to the place, or make it more generic. If you don't know the person, you must only find out their name, and write a very general note. 'Dear Steve, I knew you would select Paris. Hope you enjoy the view from the Eiffel Tower.' It's revealing their name that will impress them if they are a stranger.

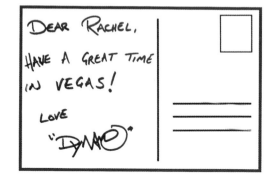

THINKING ON YOUR FEET

One of the most important skills for a magician is the ability to think on your feet and take every advantage. In 'Postcard Power', you must find out your participant's name in advance. How? The answer, of course, is that it all depends.

For example, use Facebook to look up someone's partner's name, ask the host at a party for the guest list, get a friend to tell you a guest's name (and make them promise to deny any involvement).

Years ago I performed this effect at a party for a woman I had never met. But by eavesdropping on her conversation, I knew she was about to go on her honeymoon to Orlando. One of my postcards happened to be from Orlando. I wrote on the back, 'Dear Amy: enjoy your trip and send me one of these from your honeymoon in Orlando.' She nearly burst into tears because I had made the effect so personal. I doubt I'll ever be able to repeat that performance, but it happened because I was ready to adapt.

Secret markings

2. Mark the picture side of the force card with a distinguishing mark in the top left and bottom right corners. I do this by putting a black marker dot in both corners. This way, as you spread the postcards to display them, you can easily find the force card.

PERFORMANCE
1. You're now ready to perform. Approach the participant and ask them to examine and shuffle the postcards. 'Make sure that each one is from a different place, but I'll ask you not to turn them over. There's a surprise on the back of one of those cards, and I don't want you to see it just yet.'

2. When they are done mixing, take back the stack of cards and spread them as you say, 'You shuffled these cards into an order I couldn't possibly know in advance.' As you talk, spread the cards until you approach the marked force card. Separate the cards at this point, taking the force card as the bottom card of the right-hand spread.

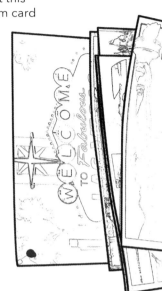

3. 'Now you're going to choose one at random.' As you say this line, gesture with your right hand, using the spread in the hand to point directly at the participant. After you gesture, place the right-hand cards to the bottom of the cards held in the left hand. This positions the force card on the bottom of the stack.

4. 'We have 20 postcards here. So name a number between one and 20.' Suppose they say, 'Nine.' Deal nine cards on to the table in a neat pile, counting as you go.

5. 'I'll mark the spot you thought of like this.' So saying, place the cards remaining in your hand on the table perpendicular to the pile on the table.

6. 'I wrote you a message on the back of one of these cards. It's for a place I think you're drawn to, whether you realise it or not. Maybe you've been to this place, or maybe it's somewhere you've always wanted to go. Let's see how we did.'

Reach down to the postcards and slowly lift up the uppermost, perpendicular packet. 'This is the exact position you named,' you say, pointing to the lowermost card of the packet you hold. Of course, this is not precisely true, but it looks like it's fair, which is all that matters.

7. Slide out the lowermost card – the force card – and display its picture. 'This is a very special place to me. And I think you'll find it's a special place for you, too. Hold on to this card for a moment.' Hand the participant the force card, but ask them not to turn it over.

8. Turn over all the other cards on the table, showing no messages written on them. 'See? You could have chosen Beijing or Tokyo or Rio or Vancouver – any of these, but you chose Las Vegas. Turn it over.' When the spectator turns over the card to discover the note you wrote to them, they will be shocked to the core.

'That postcard is yours to keep. Just promise you'll send one back to me when you get to Vegas.'

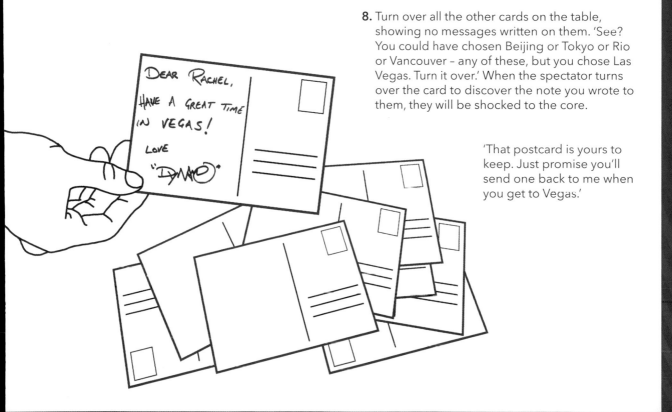

HEADLINER

EFFECT
You predict a freely-chosen word from a newspaper.

This is a mentalism effect, which is the word magicians use to describe the kind of magic that simulates mind-reading. I love mentalism because when done properly it feels authentic and pure.

OVERVIEW
You will force a predetermined word, so you know in advance which one the participant will select.

NEEDED
- Scissors
- A newspaper
- A pen
- A piece of paper and envelope

WARNING! This effect uses scissors, so it should only be attempted by adults or with adult supervision.

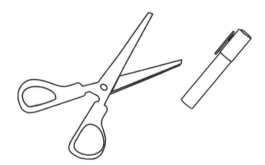

SET-UP
1. To prepare for this effect you first need to cut out a suitable article from a newspaper. Ideal articles are formatted in one long, narrow column; 5cm wide and 25cm long is ideal. Cut out this article.

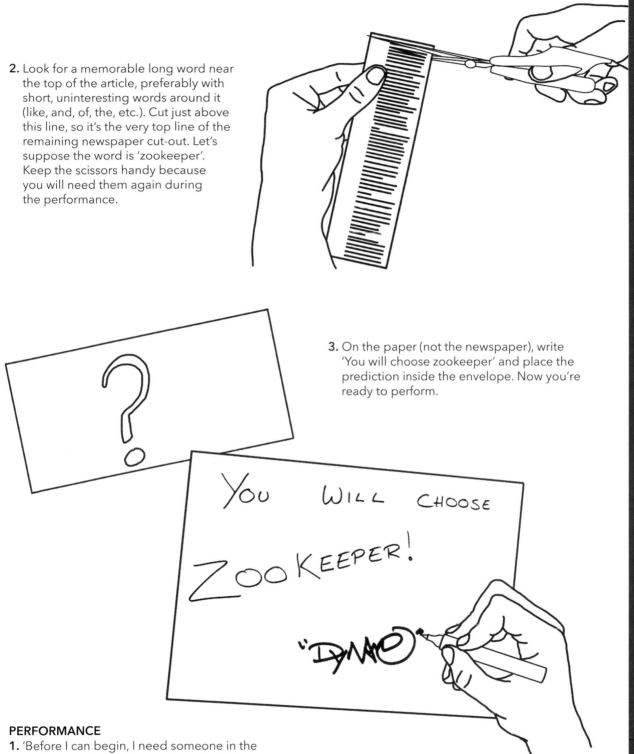

2. Look for a memorable long word near the top of the article, preferably with short, uninteresting words around it (like, and, of, the, etc.). Cut just above this line, so it's the very top line of the remaining newspaper cut-out. Let's suppose the word is 'zookeeper'. Keep the scissors handy because you will need them again during the performance.

3. On the paper (not the newspaper), write 'You will choose zookeeper' and place the prediction inside the envelope. Now you're ready to perform.

YOU WILL CHOOSE

ZOOKEEPER!

"DYNAMO"

PERFORMANCE

1. 'Before I can begin, I need someone in the audience to hold this envelope. Inside is a prediction about a word I believe someone is about to think of.' Give the envelope to someone in the audience to hold. Then invite a different person to be a participant in the effect.

2. 'I have an article with about 500 words in it. I'm going to have you select and think of one at random.' Show the article to the participant and the other spectators. Take out the scissors with your right hand and then reposition the article so that the words are facing toward you, away from the spectators. Also, reposition the article so the words are upside-down.

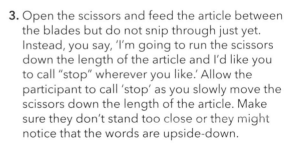

3. Open the scissors and feed the article between the blades but do not snip through just yet. Instead, you say, 'I'm going to run the scissors down the length of the article and I'd like you to call "stop" wherever you like.' Allow the participant to call 'stop' as you slowly move the scissors down the length of the article. Make sure they don't stand too close or they might notice that the words are upside-down.

'Would you like to change your mind? Go a little farther up or down?' Make sure the participant is happy with their choice.

4. At the designated spot, snip the newspaper across, so the bottom piece (which is actually the top of the upside-down article) flutters to the floor.

5. 'I don't want to see or even touch that piece. Please pick it up. Is there a word on the top line that you can make out? Go with something interesting, perhaps a long word we can have fun with. Please don't pick anything like "and" or "of" or "the". Got one?'

The spectator will pick up the fallen piece, and when they orient it right side up, it will appear to be the middle of the article. The top line will appear to be the random line they chose to stop at. They will then notice the only big word on the line, 'zookeeper,' and think of that word.

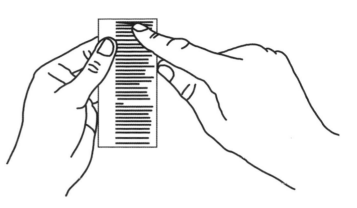

6. Now direct attention to the spectator holding the envelope. 'A few moments ago I gave someone in the audience an envelope. Remember that this was before I invited (name of spectator) to think of any word from this newspaper article. (Name of spectator), what word are you thinking of?' The spectator replies: 'Zookeeper'. Repeat the word so everybody can hear it clearly. 'Zookeeper?'

Invite the spectator in the audience to hold up the paper inside the envelope, proving that you knew exactly what the thought-of word would be.

WITH THANKS TO: This effect is often called 'Clippo' and was sold by a magician called Joseph J. Kolar in the 1920s.

SUPERHUMAN STRENGTH

EFFECT

You tell everyone that you have superhuman strength. To prove it, you hold your hands together in front of you and ask the strongest-looking person in the room to try to separate your hands… yet however hard they try, they can't!

You then pass the strength on to someone else by inviting the smallest-looking spectator to try it – and even the biggest person in the room can't separate their hands!

I find my ideas for magic in many different places, and this one isn't a magic secret at all; it's a little-known children's game that someone showed me. The bigger the size difference of the people taking part in this effect, the more hilarious it gets!

OVERVIEW

There's no real secret here as your body automatically does all the work for you. The idea of having superhuman strength is total bravado, but every effect needs a good presentation and this is a fun one.

PERFORMANCE

1. Tell a story about how you have been working out at the gym and have gained ultra strength – the more believable the story, the better the effect. Hold your hands together in front of your body, as if you were saying a prayer.

2. Ask the strongest-looking person in the room to stand directly in front of you and to hold on to your wrists.

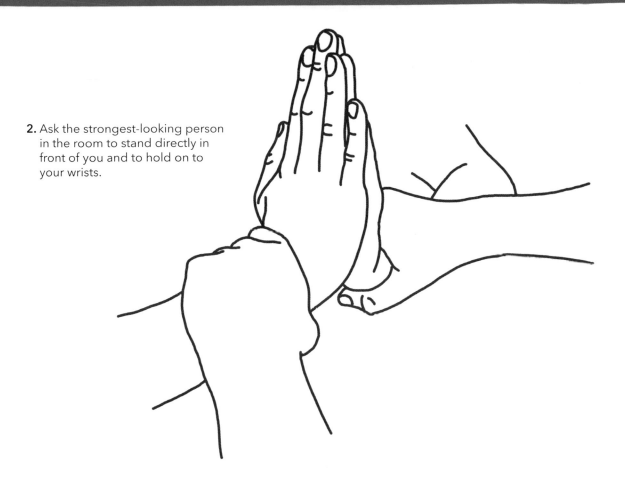

3. Explain that they must try to pull your hands apart by pulling them out to the sides. Warn them that they can't try any sneaky tactics like jerking your hands apart; they can only use their strength against yours. Amazingly, you don't even need to try – so long as you gently push your hands together, your friend won't be able to separate them! The only way that this can fail is if the participant jerks your hands apart or pulls one hand into your body and the other away from it, but you have already warned them that those tactics are considered cheating!

4. After your participant has given up, explain that you can give someone else the super strength. (It's always best if you wait until someone asks to try it because that means that they have bought into the idea that you can learn this superpower!) The piece is much more effective with a smaller person, of course, as if it's someone really strong they might be able to do this for real!

5. Tell them to hold out their hands just as you did and ask them to concentrate on pushing their palms together. Yet again, even the strongest person in the room won't be able to separate them! I find this part really fun because you don't even explain the secret of the effect to your participant and it still works!

CONNECTING MAGIC: When I used to perform this effect regularly, I used 'Superfood' (p.88) as an opener. By connecting these two routines that deal with superhuman strength, you are able to create a short but powerful themed routine.

SUPERFOOD

EFFECT
In a feat of superhuman strength, you break a borrowed apple into two pieces.

Magic effects are almost always pretending to do something impossible through secret means. But in very special cases, the magic happens exactly as it appears – it just doesn't seem possible. In 'Superfood' you appear to rip an apple into two pieces with your bare hands. And that's exactly what you do. It's easier than you might expect, but it will take some practice. If you don't get it the first time, try again – you'll get it eventually!

OVERVIEW
Although it seems impossible, with the correct leverage you can break an apple into two pieces using just your fingers and precisely applied pressure.

NEEDED
Any apple; that said, choose one that fits comfortably in your hand, and one that isn't too hard. Ripe apples work best. Remove the stem of the apple.

PERFORMANCE
1. Place the tip of your right thumb across the top of the apple, pushing as far into the recess as possible. Place your finger pads on the bottom of the apple, touching the very end.

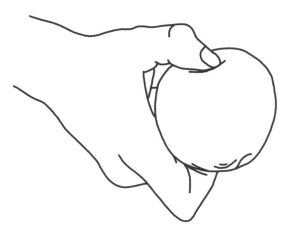

2. Place your left hand around the apple, pushing the apple into your left palm.

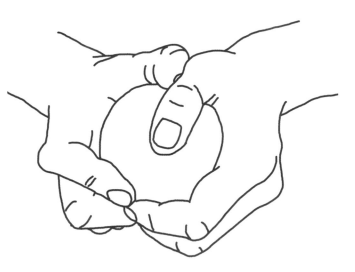

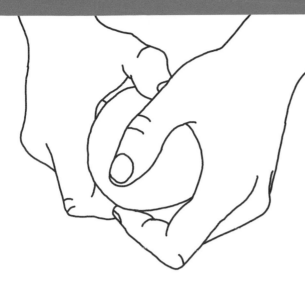

3. To brace the apple, push it against your thigh.

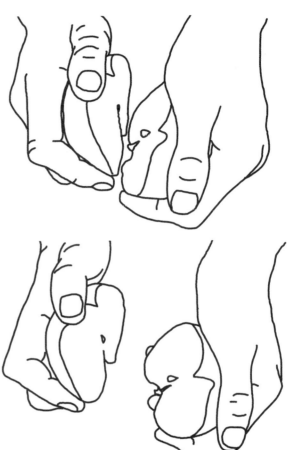

4. To rip the apple apart, begin pushing it apart by splitting it at the top. Apply firm pressure with each thumb base in opposite directions, pushing to the left with your left hand as you push to the right with your right hand.

You need to establish a back and forth rhythm of firm pressure, pulling it apart at the top and then pushing near the bottom. You'll hear a splintering sound as the apple starts to weaken along the middle.

With continuous rocking pressure, the apple will snap apart in two pieces that look like they were sliced with a knife. The apple splits with friction, not strength, so if you can't split it immediately, keep working on it. With practice you'll learn the best grip to make this happen.

AN EFFECT, NOT A TRICK

Tricks. It's a word that has always bothered me, because I detest the idea that I'm tricking someone with magic.

I use the word 'effect' to refer to the material I use, because when it's done well,

magic should affect people emotionally. The words we use make a difference, and training yourself to view magic as an effect instead of a trick is the first step toward more powerful magic.

BANANA SPLIT

EFFECT
Without touching a banana, you cut it into small pieces!

Magic can often require going to extraordinary lengths of preparation. Spectators are often fooled by their assumption that a magic effect begins when the show starts. But many of the best effects, including 'Banana Split,' rely on secret preparation.

OVERVIEW
You secretly cut the banana while it is still inside the peel. You do this using a large needle or safety pin, before the performance.

NEEDED
- A banana
- A large needle or safety pin (make sure to use one that is at least as long as the width of the banana)

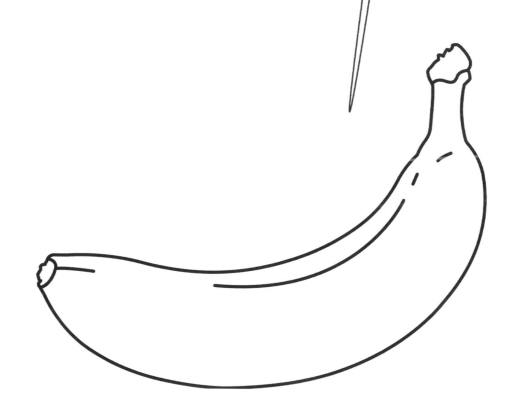

SET-UP

1. Before the performance you will put five cuts into the banana, to slice it into six segments. To make each secret cut, insert the pin through the peel of the banana, so it's not quite protruding from the opposite side. The goal is to make only a tiny prick for each cut that you make. Begin by inserting the pin about 2–3cm from the top of the banana.

2. Once the pin is inside the banana, manoeuvre it back and forth, cutting the soft interior of the banana with a width-wise incision. You don't need to worry about making the cut complete. As long as you cut through most of the fruit, the weight of each piece causes it to separate as the participant peels it.

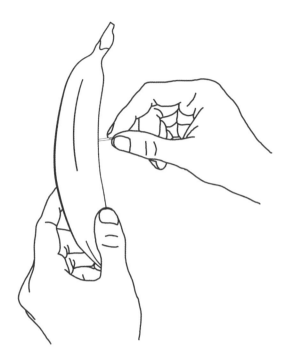

3. Insert the pin about 2–3cm down from the first pinhole, and repeat the side-to-side cutting action.

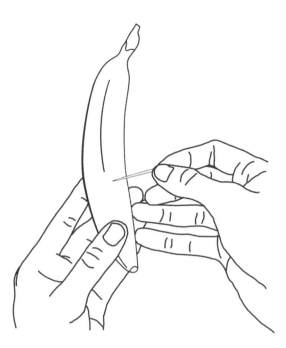

4. Continue this process down the length of the banana. The goal should be about five cuts, but if the banana you use is larger or smaller than average, you may need to adjust.

PERFORMANCE

1. The real secret to this effect is disguising the very idea that you could have prepared the banana in advance. Sneak the banana back into a fruit bowl in a public place, or on your dining room table. Wait for someone to ask you to do some magic, and then, as if making it up as you go, say: 'Okay, let's try something with, well, how about this banana?'

2. Reach for the banana and then stop yourself. 'Actually, I don't even want to touch the banana, because you might think I could do something tricky with it. So I'd like you to pick it up and hold it between your hands, like this.' Gesture for a participant to hold the banana between their palms. In this way, you're not exactly inviting them to examine the banana (because they might find the holes if they look too closely), but you are insisting that they hold the fruit, and that you never touch it.

3. 'I used to love playing charades when I was a kid. Let's try a quick game of charades.' When saying this, pretend to hold up a knife and a banana. Have people guess at what you're holding, and eventually clarify what the invisible objects are. Now mime the action of peeling the banana and cutting it into pieces. If you made five cuts during the preparation, make sure to mime a cutting action exactly five times – you would be surprised how observant spectators can be.

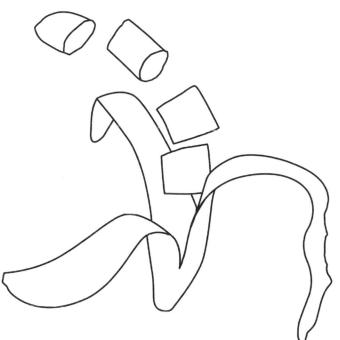

4. 'Did that look real to you? I think it was real. Peel the banana.' Invite the participant to peel the banana, cautioning them to peel it over a table (so they don't inadvertently drop the banana segments).

When the banana is peeled, it will often just fall apart into neatly cut segments. In that case, take your applause; the performance is over. But sometimes the cuts aren't quite complete, in which case the banana appears whole. These instances are even more fun. Ask the participant to pull on the banana carefully. Right before everyone's eyes, the banana will start to come apart, as if the cuts are happening invisibly, in real time.

CELEB SPOTTING

EFFECT

You show your spectators a magazine and open it to a page full of photos of celebrities. You hand it to a participant, along with a pen, and ask them to hold the magazine behind their back and to draw a circle anywhere on the page. You open your wallet to show that you have a photo of the exact celebrity the participant circled.

Here you will use a very versatile, well-kept magic secret to do all the work for you. The method is so simple that nobody would ever suspect it, and it's fully automatic!

OVERVIEW

You force the celebrity by secretly drawing the circle on the page before the effect starts. And the pen that the participant uses to draw a circle with doesn't actually write… so when they are writing behind their back, they aren't actually doing anything!

NEEDED

- A magazine full of photos of celebrities! Particularly, you need one that has a two-page spread consisting mainly of photographs; these are very common in celebrity magazines.
- A marker pen that doesn't write. The easiest way to create one is to leave the nib of the pen soaking in a cup of water for a day or two, and it'll eventually draw out all of the ink. Leave the pen to dry.
- A separate photograph of the celebrity you wish to force. This has to be a celebrity who is photographed on the two-page spread in the magazine. It should be someone that everyone immediately recognises.
- A wallet, or somewhere to place the celebrity photograph.

SET-UP

Place the extra photograph in your wallet, or somewhere that you can easily access. Then open up the magazine to the two-page spread and draw a circle around that celebrity. It's more effective if you don't fully circle the celebrity, but instead cover just two-thirds of them so that it's believable that someone could have drawn the circle behind their back. Close the magazine.

PERFORMANCE

1. Bring out the magazine and flick through some of the pages, explaining that you will use it to pick a random celebrity. As you are flicking through, casually let people see the pages of the magazine, perhaps stopping to point out photos of celebrities that you particularly like.

2. When you get to the page with your circle on it, angle the pages toward you so that nobody gets to see the circle. Fold the pages back on themselves, and hold the magazine so that the circled page is facing toward the floor.

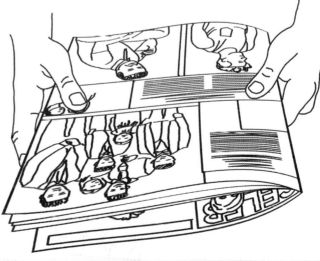

3. Ask your participant to place their hands behind their back, and then hand the magazine to them. As you do so, though, secretly turn the magazine over so that the pre-drawn circle is now facing upward. This is very easy to do; simply time it so that you can turn the magazine over when your hand goes behind their back. It's impossible for anyone to notice it!

4. Hand the no-write pen to the participant too and then explain that you want them to draw a circle anywhere on the page. Of course, they aren't actually doing anything because there is no ink in the pen!

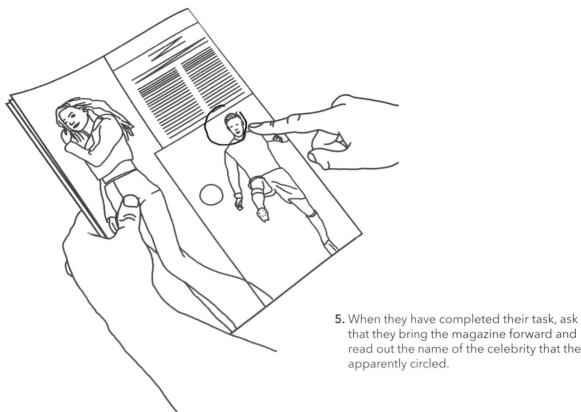

5. When they have completed their task, ask that they bring the magazine forward and read out the name of the celebrity that they apparently circled.

6. Remove the photo of the celebrity from your wallet to show that you managed to exactly predict the celebrity!

'IT ALWAYS SEEMS IMPOSSIBLE

UNTIL IT'S DONE.'

NELSON MANDELA

PART 2
THE 52 ASSISTANTS

When I started performing card magic in the streets, people told me I would never get paid to perform it. When I got paid to perform card magic, executives told me it wouldn't work on TV. When I did it on TV, producers said you can't tour stadiums with card magic, and I ended up using a piece of card magic to open my arena tours!

I think of a pack of cards like a musician regards their instrument: limitless potential.

Basics
Let's take a moment to go over the hand positions you'll need in the next chapter.

Glossary

Suits
Clubs, Hearts, Spades, Diamonds.

Value
Ace (A), 2, 3, 4, 5, 6, 7, 8, 9, 10, Jack (J), Queen (Q), King (K), Joker.

Pips
The small suit and value situated in the corner of the card.

Face
The side of the card showing the value and suits.

Back
The side of the card showing matching designs. The reverse of 'The Face'.

Shuffle
To mix the cards randomly.

Riffle Shuffle
This is a way of mixing cards on the table, and is the preferred technique in casinos worldwide. This is taught later in Part 3: Skills 101.

Squaring The Deck
Many effects tend to leave the cards in a messy (or unsquared) position. Squaring the deck means to neaten them up.

fourth

third

second

first

thumb

thumb

first

second

third

fourth

Face up

Face down

SEE-THROUGH

EFFECT
You ask someone to sit on any playing card while your back is turned. When you turn around you ask them to look up and open their mouth. You are able to look into the participant's mouth, through their body, and see what card they are sitting on.

Simple magic effects can create profound memories. 'See-Through' is extremely simple to perform, yet the premise of looking through a person is unforgettable. I used to love performing this piece for friends at parties, and they would often ask me about it years later.

OVERVIEW
You know in advance what card the participant will select.

NEEDED
A pack of cards

PERFORMANCE
1. Use any pack of cards and invite a participant sitting nearby to shuffle the cards thoroughly. 'Are you happy with this order?' you ask, as you briskly spread the cards face up to verify for everyone that the cards are mixed. Under cover of this gesture, secretly remember the top card of the deck. Let's suppose it's the Eight of Hearts.

2. 'Please cut off a small packet of cards,' you say, as you hold out the face-down deck in your outstretched left hand.

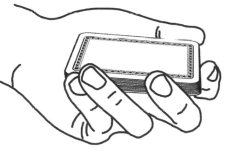

3. 'Now turn over the packet, face up, and place it back on to the deck.' Make sure they comply.

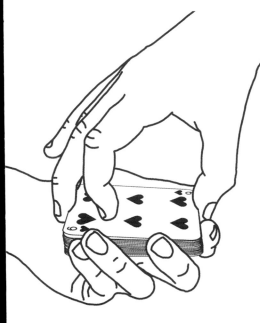

4. 'You controlled how many cards you cut off, but I can see the card you cut to, the six of Hearts, staring at us on top of the pack. So I want you to cut again, perhaps a little deeper this time, and turn over everything.' Ask the participant to cut a larger packet from your hand.

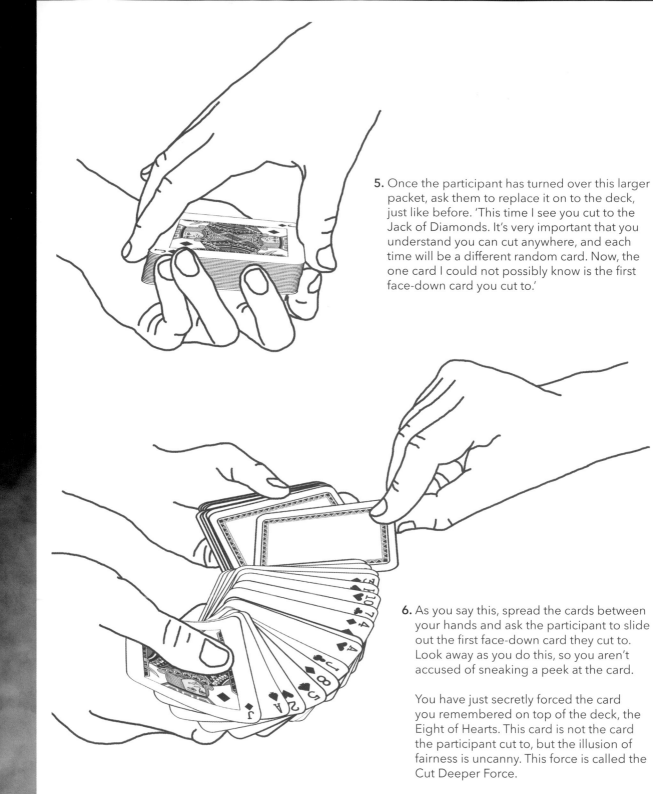

5. Once the participant has turned over this larger packet, ask them to replace it on to the deck, just like before. 'This time I see you cut to the Jack of Diamonds. It's very important that you understand you can cut anywhere, and each time will be a different random card. Now, the one card I could not possibly know is the first face-down card you cut to.'

6. As you say this, spread the cards between your hands and ask the participant to slide out the first face-down card they cut to. Look away as you do this, so you aren't accused of sneaking a peek at the card.

You have just secretly forced the card you remembered on top of the deck, the Eight of Hearts. This card is not the card the participant cut to, but the illusion of fairness is uncanny. This force is called the Cut Deeper Force.

7. From the standpoint of work, the effect is over. Now the fun begins. 'While my head is turned I want you to sit on the card. Don't look at it; just sit on it so it's out of sight. Tell me when it's safe to turn around.'

These words are carefully chosen. You want the spectator to sit on the card face down for an upcoming gag. But it's no fun if you tell them explicitly to keep it face down.

8. 'Okay, I'm going to look at the card and tell you what it is. But that's not magic… unless I look through your body. Look up at the ceiling and open your mouth.' Stand over the participant and stare deep into their mouth, shifting your head around as if you're trying to get a good view.

'Oh, I see it clearly now. But I can't tell what it is because it's face down. When I turn away, turn the card face up and then sit on it again.'

When you turn away and the participant reveals that the card is face down, this will get laughs, and even some gasps of amazement.

9. Have the spectator resume the position, and stare again 'through' their body. 'I see it's a red card, a Heart. Wait, can you just put all your weight on your left cheek? There it is! Eight of Hearts!'

Invite the participant to display the card they are sitting on to confirm and complete the illusion.

FINDING FOUR ACES

EFFECT
A participant thoroughly shuffles the deck and then places it into your pocket. By feel alone, you quickly sift through the deck (without looking) and remove the Aces, one by one.

Finding four Aces from a shuffled deck is the stuff of legends. If you're a magician, you'll get asked about it. The reason I'm including this version is because there's an important lesson in here for you. Magic often works because of assumptions the audience makes. As magicians, we take advantage of these assumptions. Here, the spectators assume that the Aces are in the deck. Bad assumption!

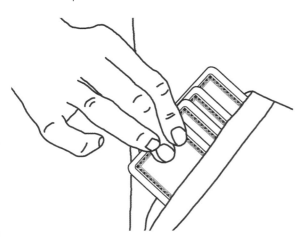

OVERVIEW
The four Aces are secretly in your pocket before the effect begins.

NEEDED
- A normal pack of cards
- A hoody or jacket with a pocket

SET-UP
1. Begin by secretly placing four Aces into your hoodie pocket with the faces closest toward your body.

PERFORMANCE
1. Hand out the pack for shuffling and invite a participant to examine the cards. Here, what you don't say is as important as what you say. You want to avoid mentioning the Aces, or anything specifically about what you intend to do. Keep it general. 'Here's a pack of cards. Make sure they're not in any particular order and then give them a very thorough shuffle.'

2. Retrieve the deck from the participant and place it in your pocket for a moment, situating the Aces already in your pocket on top of the face-down deck. Immediately retrieve all the cards from your pocket (including the Aces), as if you forgot a step. 'Actually, before I place the deck in my pocket, would you reach inside and make sure there are no extra cards or contraptions. Looks good? Empty? Great.'

The beauty of this 'mistake' is that you do exactly what you claim not to do. You load the extra cards on the deck, remove all the cards and then ask them to ensure the pocket is empty. Sneaky, right?

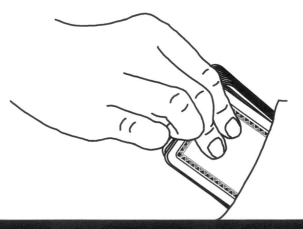

3. 'I'll place the cards into my pocket in just the order you shuffled them. And then I'll try to cut the very best cards in the deck. Which ones do you think those are?'

It sounds like you're offering the participant a choice of what cards they 'think' would be the best. But of course, you will find the Aces. Most often, the participant will name the Aces. In this case, act as if they could have named any cards. 'You want Aces? Okay, we'll find Aces then.'

If the participant names something else, politely correct them. 'Actually, Aces are even higher than Queens, so we'll look for Aces.'

4. The rest of the effect is just acting. Reach into your pocket and fumble a bit, as if searching through the pack for one card that somehow feels like an Ace. With your thumb, riffle the corners of the pack to make what sounds like shuffling through the cards in search of the right one. Pull out the top card and reveal it dramatically.

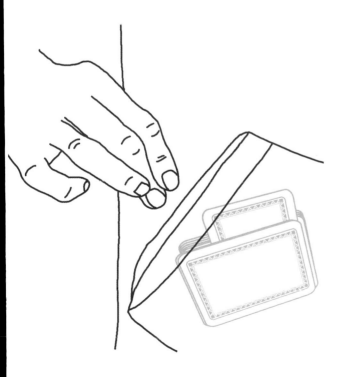

5. Repeat this process two more times, finding a total of three Aces. Before you remove the third Ace, you will do a secret task in your pocket. Take the fourth Ace from the top of the deck and turn it perpendicular to the other cards, so that it sticks out about 2–3cm above the rest. Insert the card into the middle of the deck in this perpendicular position, so that it sticks out above the other cards.

6. 'Perhaps you think finding the Aces by feel is easy. Trust me, it's REALLY hard. Go ahead. You try! Just reach into my pocket and pull out a card as fast as you can.' So saying, invite the participant to reach into your pocket and pull out a card. Rush them in this task, and the result is one of two outcomes: they will either go for the first card they feel, which is the perpendicular final Ace, or they won't!

If they go for the Ace, you have a miracle! Ask them to display the card and to take a bow of their own. If the participant takes any other card, play it off like a gag. 'See? I told you it was hard!' Now reach into your pocket and remove the Ace yourself, bringing the effect to a successful conclusion.

MAGICIAN'S ASSISTANT

EFFECT
Ever wanted to have me do a card effect for you?
How about me helping you with a card effect.
You invite a participant to select a card from the
pack, and then play a video of me on your mobile.
Together, we'll manage to find the chosen card!

It means everything to me that you're studying
magic, and letting me share some of my favourite
effects. Since I can't possibly meet and perform
with all of you live, I've created this illusion so we
can, in a way, do magic together.

OVERVIEW
You will force the Two of Clubs, and then play
a video I've already made for you, in which we,
together, find the Two for the participant.

NEEDED
– A pack of cards
– A smartphone with the ability to play video

SET-UP
1. Cue up the video I made for you at
dynamomagician.com/secrets.
If you play the video, you'll understand that with
a bit of acting you produce the Two of Clubs.
You will need to have the video ready to play.

In your pack of cards, place the Two of Clubs on
top. In a moment you will perform the Cross-Cut
Force from p.30-31. Familiarise yourself with this
sequence before proceeding.

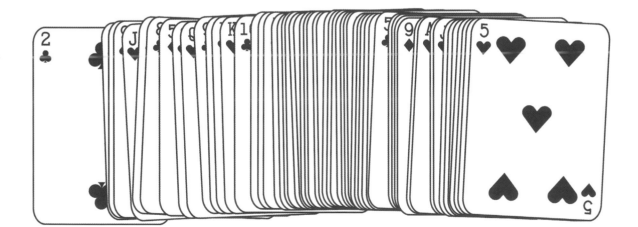

PERFORMANCE

1. Begin by saying, 'In this next effect I'm going to have you pick a card. So cut the pack anywhere you like.' Begin the actions of the Cross-Cut Force. Mark the place they cut by placing the lower half on top of the upper packet, crosswise.

2. 'But I'm not going to find your card. For that, I'll need Dynamo. Sadly, he couldn't be with us here today, but he can still help us find your card. Speaking of your card, please remember the one you cut to.' Here, you help slide out the upper card on the lower packet and invite the participant to look at the card, remember it and place it back into the deck anywhere.

3. Now play the video on your phone. I'll talk for a moment and then instruct the spectator to place their hand on top of the phone, covering the screen.

Be careful that when your spectator covers the screen, they don't accidentally press the screen or hit a button!

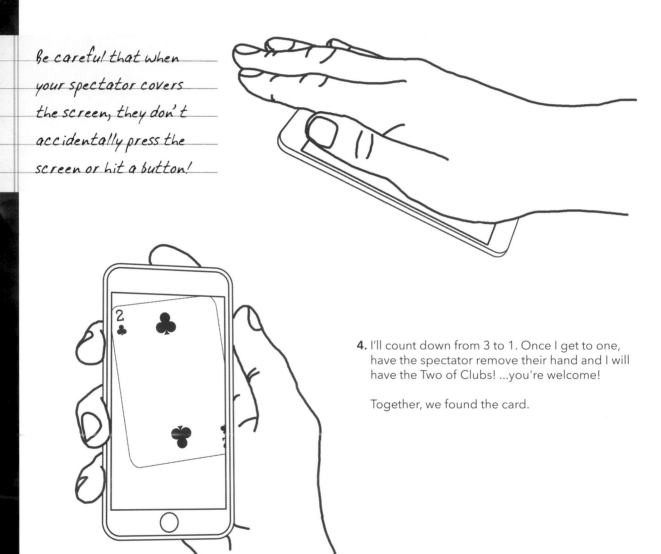

4. I'll count down from 3 to 1. Once I get to one, have the spectator remove their hand and I will have the Two of Clubs! ...you're welcome!

Together, we found the card.

Like any performer I stand on the shoulders of giants. David Berglas really changed the way people create and think about magic. The 'International Man of Mystery' is a master of the art and has influenced some of the worlds greatest modern magicians.

WALLET WONDER

EFFECT

Eight cards are displayed and a participant is asked to select one. The one they touch proves to be the only red card in the packet; all the other cards have blue backs!

I have included this effect because I want you to have something you can carry with you at all times. I used to carry this effect in my wallet, so I could do it at any moment, without any notice. It packs flat but plays big.

OVERVIEW

Half the cards are blue and the other half are red. Depending on which card is touched, you can use a sneaky display to show all the cards are blue except for one red, or all the cards are red except for one blue.

NEEDED

- Any four cards from a red-backed deck
- Any four cards from a blue-backed deck

SET-UP

1. Make sure that all eight cards you use are different, representing a variety of suits and values. Also take care that the fronts of the cards from each deck appear uniform; some stylised decks have artwork and colouration on the faces that give away the back design. Classic designs of red and blue cards work best.

Alternate the back designs of the cards. From the front the spread looks normal. From the back, it looks ridiculous.

2. Store this packet of cards in your wallet, handbag or pocket.

PERFORMANCE

1. When you're ready to perform, remove the packet face up, being careful not to reveal the colours on the backs of the cards. Spread the fan of cards widely so the spectators can see the value of each one.

'This is the thinnest deck of cards in the world. Every time I do the effect, it gets thinner by exactly one card. That's because there's one card here that doesn't belong. I want you to look over each card and then touch the one you think is different.'

2. When the participant touches a card, separate the fan at the touched card, cutting this card to the top of the packet.

3. Deal the touched card on to the table, or on to the participant's hand. 'That's the one you think is different from all the others.'

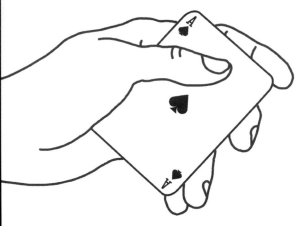

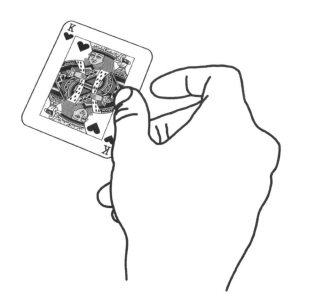

4. You will now apparently show the backs of all the other cards. Actually, you will carry out a clever display that conceals all the other cards matching the one the participant touched. Let's suppose they touched a red card, which is now face up in the participant's hand. This means that there is a blue card on the face and rear of the face-up packet in your hand. The illustration shows the underside of the packet, which the audience never sees.

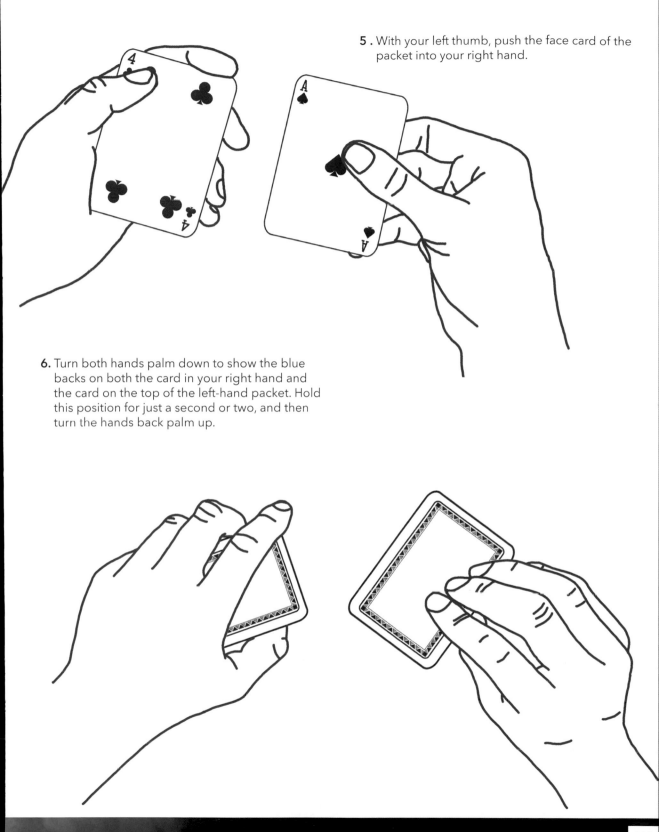

5 . With your left thumb, push the face card of the packet into your right hand.

6. Turn both hands palm down to show the blue backs on both the card in your right hand and the card on the top of the left-hand packet. Hold this position for just a second or two, and then turn the hands back palm up.

7. Drop the card in your right hand on to the table as you thumb over the top card of the left-hand packet and deal it, face up, on top of the tabled card.

It appears as if you have shown the backs of two cards and dealt them on to the table. Actually, you showed the back of the entire left-hand packet and passed it off as the back of the face card. Done with confidence, this discrepancy is never perceived.

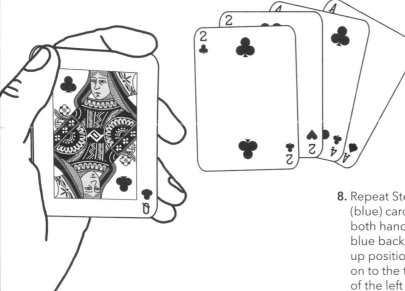

WITH THANKS TO: *This classic of magic is often called 'Eight-Card Brainwave' and is the invention of Nick Trost.*

8. Repeat Steps 6–8 by thumbing over the top (blue) card into your right hand, and turning both hands palm down to display two more blue backs, then returning the cards to a face-up position. Deal the right-hand card face up on to the tabled pile and then the face card of the left hand's packet. Again, it appears as if you have shown two more blue cards. With proper rhythm it should look as if you deal the two cards on to the table almost simultaneously, even though the right hand's card always drops to the table first.

9. Repeat this display sequence yet again to show two more blue-backed cards. You'll be left with a single blue card in your left hand. Show it front and back and deal it on to the pile.

Not only does this clever sequence show all the cards as blue, but it resets the cards into alternating blue/red order for your next performance.

10. 'Turn over your card. I told you it was different!' The participant can turn over the card in their hand to reveal that they apparently selected the only red card.

HECKLERS

Magicians always ask me how I deal with hecklers. The truth is, I don't. If someone is being aggressive toward your magic, one of two things has occurred:

1. You are performing for someone you shouldn't, so stop immediately. If they don't respect your magic, don't bother trying to entertain them.

2. You are somehow challenging or antagonising the audience, even if you don't realise it. In this case, you must soften your approach or be more respectful to your audience.

To stop hecklers, you have to understand them. Hecklers want attention, so it's best to give it to them! Perhaps they want to be the star of a trick? In this case, perform something like 'Coincealed' on p.60 or 'Postcard Power' on p.76, where the participant gets part of the credit. Rather than confronting them, acknowledge their presence, laugh at the jokes (which are almost never funny) and keep the performance moving.

MOBILE MAGIC

EFFECT
You invite a participant to shuffle packets of cards face up and face down, creating a big mess. Unexpectedly, the participant precisely shuffles the pack so that all the face-up cards correspond to your mobile phone number!

In this notebook I've made an effort to modernise the magic I develop. Here I have taken a great but simple card effect, and added a mobile phone into the mix. This modern twist updates the effect for today's audiences.

NEEDED
- A pack of cards
- Your mobile and a friend's mobile

SET-UP
1. Before you begin, set the deck with cards that correspond to your mobile number. Make sure the number reads from the back to the face of the packet. So if your mobile number is 07759 645072, the packet should look like the photo. Note that for zeros you can use Queens (which have a Q in the corner that looks like a zero).

2. Place this packet on the face of the deck and have your phone handy. Now you're ready to begin.

PERFORMANCE

1. 'I'll show you something but I have to do it sort of fast because I'm expecting a call.' As you talk, place your mobile on the table off to the side, out of the way. Make sure the ringer is on. Spread the deck face up and take all the cards that correspond to your mobile number into your right hand.

2. Place these cards in a face-down pile on the table to your left. Then spread another ten to 15 cards into your right hand.

3. Place these cards in a pile face up to the right of the pile already on the table.

4. Spread over another ten to 15 cards into your right hand.

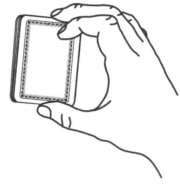

5. Place these cards into a face-down pile to the right of the other two piles.

6. Finally, take all the remaining cards and table them face up to the right of the other three piles.

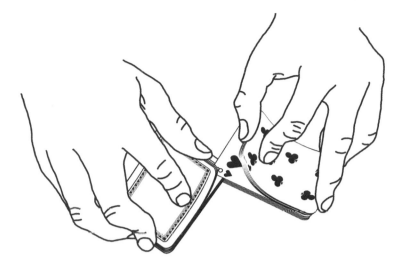

7. 'Do you know how to do a riffle shuffle?' Find a participant familiar with cards, and invite them to help. 'I'd like you to shuffle the cards for me, but in a special way. I want you to shuffle face-up cards into face-down cards to create a mess.' So saying, push the two packets to your left toward the participant and ask them to shuffle them together. They must use a riffle shuffle at this stage.

8. Take back the combined, shuffled packet from the participant and say, 'Great. Now you'll do it again, mixing face up and face down.' As you talk, turn over the combined packet and push this packet and the one to your right (which is face up) toward the participant. Although one packet is slightly larger than the other, invite the participant to riffle shuffle the packets together.

Although this process seems fair and haphazard, you will notice that after this second shuffle, only the mobile-stacked packet is reversed in the large packet.

9. Take back the combined packet and again turn it over. This is easy to remember because after every shuffle, you must turn over the combined packet.

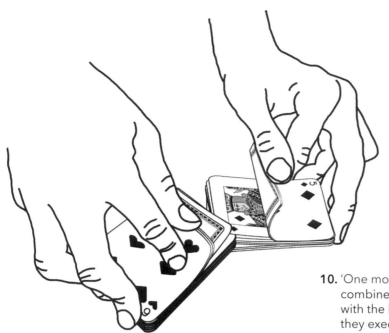

10. 'One more shuffle, please.' So saying, push the combined packet toward the spectator, along with the last remaining (face-up) packet. After they execute the last riffle shuffle, square up everything and turn over the entire pack. Now only the mobile-stack is face up; all the other cards are face down.

11. Place the pack on the table to your right and spread the cards widely to the left. This way, the sequence will read right side up to your spectators.

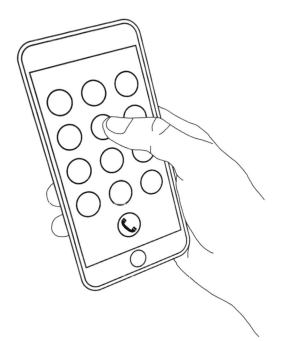

12. 'Now take out your mobile for me, and if you can do this quickly, I'm expecting a call soon from someone really important. I want you to key in the numbers that have randomly come up by your shuffling. So it starts with a 3, then Ace would be 1, then a Two, then I guess we can call Queens a zero since they look like a zero…'

Continue in this fashion until they have keyed in all the numbers of your mobile. You can recount the fair conditions of the effect – that THEY did all the shuffling, face up and face down.

13. Ask them to hit 'send' and just wait. Your mobile will ring and people will immediately realise that they somehow shuffled randomly to your mobile number, and that the important call you've been waiting for all along is from the participant.

CREDIT: The amazing shuffle sequence that allows this effect to work is a simplified version of a beautiful idea by John Bannon called 'Play It Straight Triumph'.

THE DREAM CARD

EFFECT
A participant deals through the deck, and amazingly stops at a card you predicted in advance.

The card magic I'm drawn to is the sort you can perform for anyone, at any time, with any borrowed deck, which is the case with 'The Dream Card'. For many years this was one of my go-to effects, and I'm pleased to share it with you now.

OVERVIEW
Although the conditions are extremely fair, you will secretly control what card the participant selects by glancing at the two bottom cards of the pack.

NEEDED
A pack of cards

PERFORMANCE
1. A feature of this effect is that it can be done with any deck and absolutely no preparation. So if possible, borrow the deck. If not, use your own pack but encourage a participant to shuffle it before you begin. Then take the deck and spread it so only you can see the faces.

   'I had a dream about a card effect last night. You shuffled the cards and then dealt two random cards. Using those two cards you created a playing card. And I remember your card from my dream.' As you talk, turn over the first two cards. You will use these two cards to create a card; you'll use the value of the first card and the suit of the second card. For example, if the card on the face is the Seven of Hearts and the next card is the Three of Clubs, you would remember the Seven of Clubs. If you see the Ten of Diamonds and the Six of Spades, you would remember the Ten of Spades. Let's assume you see the Eight of Clubs and the Six of Hearts.

   Sometimes there are two cards of matching suits or values. In this rare event, the effect won't work. But don't worry, the fix is simply to cut the deck casually and try again.

2. Keep spreading through the deck until you come to the card you remembered, in this case the Eight of Hearts - as you saw the Eight of Clubs and the Six of Hearts. Take it out but don't show it around. Instead, place it onto the table or on top of a glass - anywhere that the spectators can keep an eye on it.

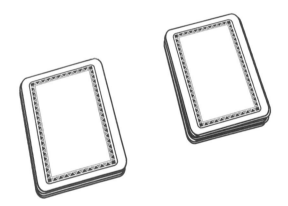

3. 'That's the one you selected in my dream. Now, in the dream you took the deck back and cut two packets to the table, one here and one here.' Hand the deck back to the participant and invite them to cut a small packet to the table, and then another one next to it. They should have some cards left over in their hands.

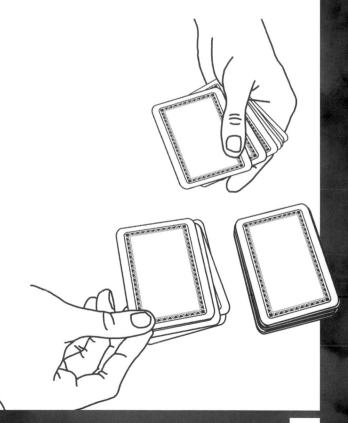

4. 'That's exactly how you cut the cards in the dream!' Continue, 'Since you cut the cards, you have determined the starting point to deal from. I want you to deal the cards back and forth, one by one, until they're all gone.'

Invite the participant to choose whether to start on the left or right pile and have them deal cards which remained in their hand singly, onto the two piles, alternating piles, until all the cards are exhausted.

5. Despite the freedom to cut anywhere, and the choice to start on the left or right, the last two cards dealt will be the two you remembered on the face of the pack.

6. Ask the spectator to turn over the top card on each pile. 'That's just how you did it in the dream. And in the dream we used these two cards to create a playing card. We'll take the value from one card and the suit from the other. That's an Eight and that's a Heart. So you've created the Eight of Hearts, just like in my dream…'

7. Turn over the card you removed at the beginning to bring this magical dream to an end.

WITH THANKS TO: The inspiration for this effect, 'The Dream Card', comes from an influential magician named Daryl Martinez, who recently passed away. He was an inspiration to myself and all other magicians, and he'll be missed.

DARYL

When I first started getting into card magic, I heard about a magician named Daryl who had just won first place in card magic at FISM (which is like the Olympics of magic). He released a video called 'The Encyclopaedia Of Card Sleights' and I saved up all my earnings from my paper round so I could buy it. Once I had a copy, I made it my mission to learn the magic inside out and back to front so I could be as good as my newfound idol, Daryl.

In 2000 I visited my grandma in Memphis, Tennessee and while I was there I heard that Daryl was lecturing at the local magic

society! Frustratingly I discovered that I wasn't old enough to attend the lecture as it was in a bar that was for over 21s only. The next morning I was still disappointed so my grandma and grandpa took me out for brunch. Suddenly, I got a tap on shoulder and when I turned around, I saw it was Daryl! My grandparents had arranged for us to have brunch together as they could see how upset I was. He was so generous with his time and spent the whole afternoon with me sharing his incredible wisdom. One particular piece of advice stays with me to this day – be patient when learning magic.

SWEET!

EFFECT
You ask a participant to shuffle the cards thoroughly as you make a friendly wager: if you fail to amaze them, you'll give them a chocolate bar. The effect appears to go wrong until you point out that they have shuffled the cards into the precise order to match the numbers on the barcode on the chocolate bar. Sweet!

One of the issues I find with magic is that it's hard to play a superhero all the time. That is, it eventually gets boring if every effect I do is just another display of how I'm magic and the audience isn't. This is why I often develop more subtle ways to reveal an illusion. In 'Sweet!' it isn't me 'doing' the magic, but instead it's a spooky, amazing coincidence.

OVERVIEW
A mathematical principle allows the participant to shuffle the cards twice without disturbing the order of ten cards. These ten cards are preset in the order of the numbers of the barcode you wish to use.

NEEDED
- A pack of cards
- A chocolate bar or pack of sweets that contains a barcode with no repeating numbers, and no letters. The barcode should also have nine numbers or fewer. This is easy to sort if you spend a few minutes in a sweet shop. Or, you can use the bottle and label from 'H2Oooooo' (p.28).

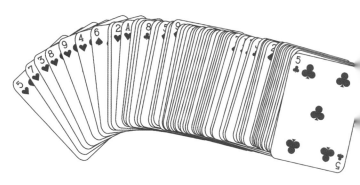

SET-UP
Using only the Hearts cards in the pack, duplicate the barcode number on top of the pack, with the first number on top, the second number second from top, and so on. Obviously, you won't use the court cards, nor will every Heart card be used. But set only the Hearts required for the barcode on top of the deck. Remove the others from the pack entirely. Now you're ready to perform.

PERFORMANCE
1. 'Let's make a friendly wager on the next effect. You can have this chocolate bar if the effect doesn't go right. I'll place it here for now.' Set the chocolate bar on the table and continue.

2. 'Before we begin, it's important you shuffle the deck. Do you know a riffle shuffle?' You must use a participant who knows how to do a proper riffle shuffle. Divide the deck roughly in half and ask the participant to shuffle the packets together.

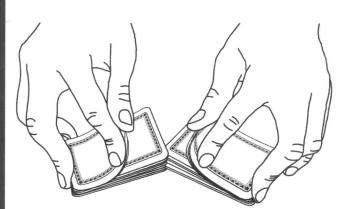

3. Now divide the deck as close to evenly in half as possible, and invite them to shuffle the packets again. 'Now you've shuffled the deck twice and I haven't touched the cards. I'm not going to touch them for the rest of the effect.'

Despite the two legitimate shuffles, amazingly, the Heart cards you preset on top of the deck are still in order. It's just that now there are some cards between them.

4. 'In this effect we only need the Hearts. Now, the pack might not be full, but remove the Hearts as you come to them, and place them into a pile here, on the table.' Invite the participant to pick up the pack and to spread it face up, taking out each Heart that they come to and placing it into a face-up pile on the table. It's important that they remove all the Hearts in the order they find them, so encourage them to go slowly, so they don't miss any.

5. 'Do these cards mean anything to you? No? Well, then I guess you win the chocolate. Unless…' Pick up the chocolate bar, and as you go to hand it over, apparently notice the barcode.

'Wait a minute. This is so weird. You shuffled the deck, and I haven't touched the cards. But read out the numbers, one by one, on the barcode.'

6. As the participant calls out the numbers, deal through the face-up pile to show that the numbers perfectly correspond, creating an unlikely miracle. Now it's up to you whether you give out the chocolate bar, or keep it for yourself!

WITH THANKS TO: The amazing shuffle sequence used in 'Sweet!' was popularised by Charles Jordan in 1919.

TRUE MATES

EFFECT

You give a couple or two friends half the deck each. They then select cards and you place their card back into the deck in a secret place. Even though the two participants didn't see where you put the cards in the deck, they're able to find each other's selected cards!

What if a card effect could go deeper than the surface level? This is an effect that I only perform for couples, because that's what makes it more than just a trick: it's about two people connecting and finding each other, but it can also work with just two close friends. Perform it for the right people and I think you'll see why it has become one of the most impactful card illusions that I perform.

OVERVIEW

By secretly placing the participants' cards in a specific place in the deck you are able to make sure that they always find their cards. It's a clever, and bold, misdirection that is impossible to deconstruct.

NEEDED

A pack of cards

PERFORMANCE

1. We'll assume that you are performing for a couple, like a husband and wife, but it can be any two people who are close. The effect is even better if you are stood in front of a table and the couple are sat at either end, looking at each other. Shuffle your cards and spread them out face down on the table in a vertical spread between them.

2. Invite both the husband and wife to remove a card from the spread and then to look at it. Make a big deal out of the fact that they should not show their cards to each other because in a moment they are going to find their partner's card.

3. While the couple are remembering their cards, pick up the rest of the deck and square them in your hand. Hold the cards behind your back and say, 'This isn't about the cards; it's about both of you. You are going to find each other's cards. I am going to place your cards somewhere in the deck but it is important that you don't see where so I'll do it behind my back. You'll then have to find each other's cards!'

4. Take the husband's card without looking at it, and place it behind your back. Act as though you are putting the card in the middle of the deck, but really put it on the bottom of the deck.

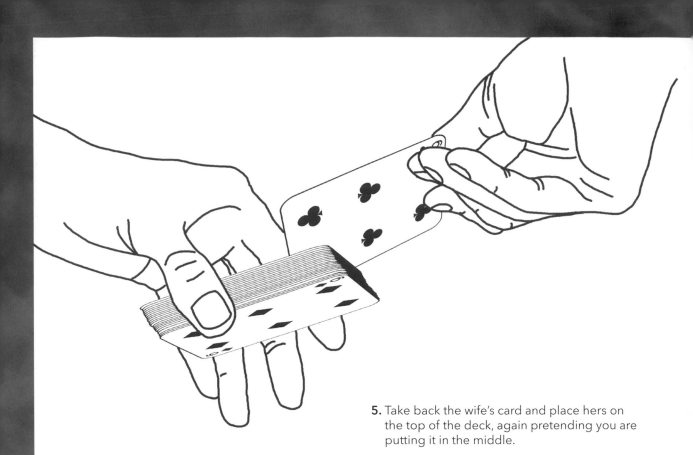

5. Take back the wife's card and place hers on the top of the deck, again pretending you are putting it in the middle.

6. Bring the cards back in front of you and ask if the participants have their driving licences on them. If they don't, you can improvise with something like a credit card, a banknote or even just a piece of paper with their name written on it. Ask them to swap driving licences so that the husband has his wife's, and vice versa. They will use the licences to find each other's cards.

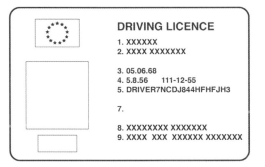

DRIVING LICENCE

1. XXXXXX
2. XXXX XXXXXXX

3. 05.06.68
4. 5.8.56   111-12-55
5. DRIVER7NCDJ844HFHFJH3

7.

8. XXXXXXXX XXXXXXX
9. XXXX XXX XXXXXX XXXXXXX

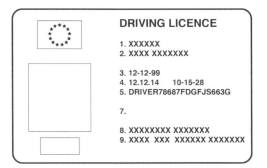

DRIVING LICENCE

1. XXXXXX
2. XXXX XXXXXXX

3. 12-12-99
4. 12.12.14   10-15-28
5. DRIVER78687FDGFJS663G

7.

8. XXXXXXXX XXXXXXX
9. XXXX XXX XXXXXX XXXXXXX

7. Hand the wife the deck of cards and ask her to deal the cards one by one face down on to the table. As she is doing this, her husband must look her in the eye and ask her to stop when he feels that she has dealt her card. Obviously nobody can actually see the cards as they are face down, so he must apparently use his intuition to stop her at the right point.

8. Once she has been stopped, ask the wife to place the driving licence on top of the pile on the table and then to place the remainder of the deck on top.

9. Ask the husband to pick up the deck and repeat the exact same thing: he must deal cards on to the table one by one and then the wife must stop when she thinks his card has been dealt. She must then place his driving licence on top, before he finally places the rest of the deck on top.

10. Believe it or not, the two spectators have somehow found each other's cards. It sounds impossible, but the effect really has worked itself and you're about to see how! Spread the cards along the table and point out the two driving licences. Remove each licence, and the cards directly above them. Turn each one over and show that the two participants magically found their partner's cards. They really were meant to find each other.

WITH THANKS TO: The basis of this effect comes from Karl Fulves, who called the effect 'Gemini Mates'. The idea of two people finding their partner's card comes from Allan Zola Kronzek from the USA.

It's worth remembering that magic lives in the mind of the spectator and not in the hand of the magician. The first time you experience a moment of pure astonishment it will live with you forever!

HOME-MADE DECK

EFFECT

A home-made deck of cards is displayed: it's a deck made from index cards, with drawings of each card on one side. Someone selects one of these home-made cards, but you fail to find it. To redeem yourself, you knock all the index cards out of the participant's hand, and cause the actual chosen playing card to appear between the participant's fingers.

This effect has an interesting, believable story behind it, which is part of its charm. The best magic exceeds the audience's wildest expectations of how it can end. In 'Home-made Deck' you offer to find the home-made playing card. But when the actual playing card appears in the participant's hand, it catches absolutely everyone off-guard.

OVERVIEW

You force the home-made Three of Hearts on a participant and, using a little-known property of playing cards, you are able to sneak in the real Three of Hearts between their fingers.

NEEDED

- 3" x 5" index cards
- Coloured markers
- A Three of Hearts playing card
- A rubber band

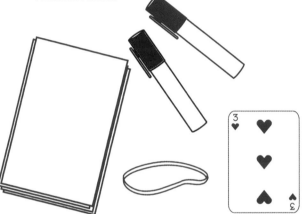

SET-UP

1. The one-time preparation for 'Home-made Deck' will take you 30 minutes, but then the reset time between performances is quite fast. To begin, you need to make a 'home-made' deck from your stack of index cards. On the blank side of each one, draw the design of each card. It's okay if they look home-made – they're supposed to!

2. On the other side, use a pen to scrawl in notes as if these cards have been used in a speech or to remember things from a class you took. This step is optional but adds authenticity.

3. When you have completed drawing the deck, situate the hand-drawn Three of Hearts in the middle of the stack. Insert the real Three of Hearts face down just beneath the hand-drawn Three of Hearts.

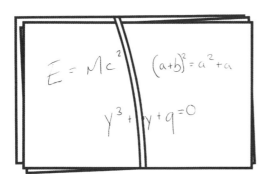

4. Wrap the entire stack in a rubber band. Now you're ready to perform.

PERFORMANCE

1. 'I started doing magic when I was in school but they don't allow students to have playing cards. So I got cheeky and made my own. This way I could do magic for friends and practise at school without ACTUALLY using playing cards.'

Remove the rubber band from the pack and show the top few cards, front and back. Take care not to expose the real Three of Hearts in the middle.

2. 'I'll try one of my favourites from my schooldays for you now. The only problem is that every time I did this effect, I would get detention at school for breaking the rules and you will see why. Let's do it. Remember one from the middle.'

So saying, riffle the outer end of the home-made deck and angle the faces of the index cards to the participant. They will see the cards flicker by quickly. There will be a natural stop when you riffle to the real Three of Hearts because it's smaller and a different shape to all the other cards. Allow your fingers to stop riffling when you reach this card.

3. The real Three will be hidden against the card that rests beneath it, but the participant will be able to see the hand-drawn Three of Hearts. Ask them to remember this card. 'Got it. Keep that card in mind and don't forget it.'

4. Say, 'Form your hand into a fist, with the thumb on top, like this.' Gesture for the participant to hold their hand like yours.

5. 'We won't use all the cards, but rather just a few you might have selected.' Place the top card under their thumb, against their fist.

6. Slide several more cards from the top under their thumb, always placing the index cards under the index cards already under their thumb. Place each notecard in at a different angle to create a big, messy fan of cards.

7. Riffle gently to the middle of the pack, where the real Three of Hearts secretly resides. Carefully take all the index cards above the real Three, along with the Three. Make sure the playing card rides beneath the other cards without poking out at all. Hold these cards in your right hand, as a stack.

8. Place all the cards, as a stack, under the fan of index cards in the participant's hand. They won't realise it, but the lowermost card of them all is now the real Three of Hearts.

9. 'I'll try and hit your card out of the stack.' Make sure the participant has a firm grip on the cards. Hold your right hand out flat, with the palm facing down.

10. In one swift motion, smack the index cards from the participant's hand. With proper force, all of them will fall to the floor except the lowermost, real Three of Hearts. This is a stunning moment because a real playing card seems to appear in their hand.

If some of the cards don't fall on your first attempt, quickly smack again. The real Three is in no danger of falling because the friction against the participant's skin will keep it in place as the others fall.

11. 'What card did you select? The Three of Hearts? Turn it over.' The participant reveals that the card in their hand is the Three of Hearts, and you end by saying, 'But then I'd end up in detention because there is a rule against having playing cards in school!'

WITH THANKS TO: My friend Joshua Jay created 'Home-made Deck' and it's a perfect effect to share with friends, particularly if you're young and still at school.

INSTANT KINGS

EFFECT

A participant selects a card (say, the King of Hearts) and you then show your elite cardsharp abilities by finding the other three Kings in increasingly impressive ways. The fun part is that the effect doesn't use any sleight of hand at all and is actually very easy!

I have always loved card magic and have spent many years practising it, since I was young. Many of the effects that I perform have taken years of practice but this one is designed to look extremely difficult, even though it is actually very easy! In fact, it's so easy that it's almost automatic – most of the time you don't even know where the Kings are yourself until you find them!

OVERVIEW

Before the effect begins, the Kings are positioned in the deck, making them very easy for you to find – so easy in fact, that the participant finds the first one without realising that you're forcing it on them (we've seen forces in other effects in this book, and you'll learn yet another one in this effect).

NEEDED

A pack of cards

SET-UP

Place one of the Kings inside the card box and leave that on the table. Then put the other three Kings on top of the deck, with the second and third Kings secretly turned over. The audience won't be aware that they are reversed (or face up, as magicians call it) because the topmost King is the correct way round.

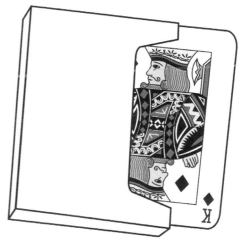

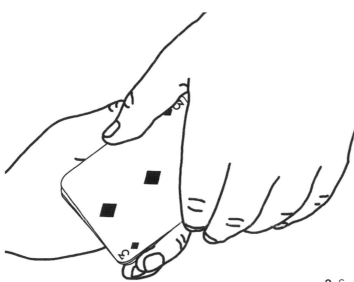

PERFORMANCE

1. Hold the deck so that the backs are facing upward and ask a participant to cut off any number of cards, then turn them over and put them back on top of the deck.

2. Spread through the cards to show all the face-up cards. Say, 'You could have cut to any of these face-up cards, but you didn't. You cut to this one here.' Stop as soon as you reach the first face-down card. That's the card that the participant apparently selected (really it's one of the reversed Kings that you set up at the start – it's a very clever force that even fools me as I do it on myself!).

3. Take all of the face-up cards into your right hand and give your participant the first face-down card. Ask them to show everyone (including you) the card. It will be a King. It's apparently a random card, but really you have forced it.

4. Turn the face-up cards in your right hand back face down on to the deck. Explain, 'I will now attempt to find the other three Kings from this deck. It will require some difficult sleight of hand, but I think I can do it!'

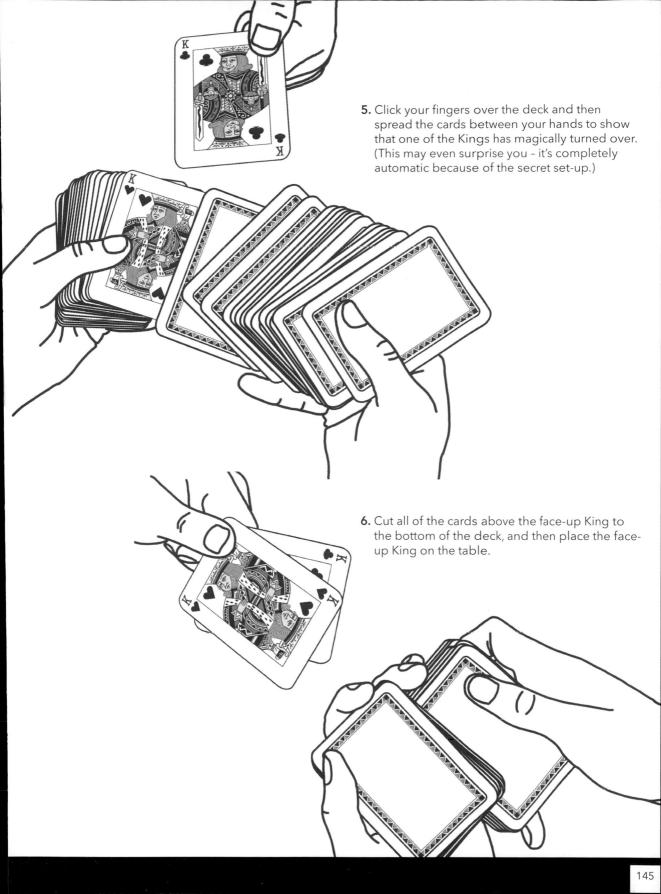

5. Click your fingers over the deck and then spread the cards between your hands to show that one of the Kings has magically turned over. (This may even surprise you – it's completely automatic because of the secret set-up.)

6. Cut all of the cards above the face-up King to the bottom of the deck, and then place the face-up King on the table.

7. The next King is found in such a simple way, but even people watching closely won't realise. Simply turn the deck over, end for end, as you say, 'The next King is right here.' You're just showing the King that is on the bottom of the deck, but as you've just cut the cards, it seems impossible!

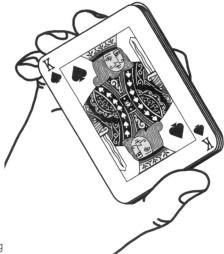

8. Finally, click your fingers over the card box and then shake it so that people can hear something instead. Remove the last King from the box and everyone will think that you have crazily good cardsharp skills!

ADAPT
APPLY
ASTONISH

In this book you have learned many different secret magic principles such as forces (like the one in this effect), secret set-ups (such as in 'Finding Four Aces', p.106), and gimmicks (such as the one in 'Card in Shoe', on the next page). The best magicians find ways to apply these principles to other effects. For example, you might want to make a card appear under your hat by forcing it using the technique described here, and then find it by secretly putting a duplicate of that card in your hat before you start the effect.

The effects in this book are just the starting point – I hope that you will be creative and find ways to create your own ideas using these secret magic moves and principles.

CARD IN SHOE

EFFECT
You cause a spectator's selected card to appear in your shoe!

A recent scientific study about magic has confirmed what I have known through experience to be true: that card magic is more memorable when it involves something else, along with the cards. People are unable to describe what happens in most card effects shortly after viewing them. The great news is that their recall improves dramatically if there's another "thing" used in the effect. Here, the other thing is a shoe, and the impact is devastating.

OVERVIEW
You force the selected card on a participant and reveal a pre-placed duplicate in your shoe.

NEEDED
– Your shoe
– A pack of cards
– An extra Two of Spades (or any card)
– Strong glue

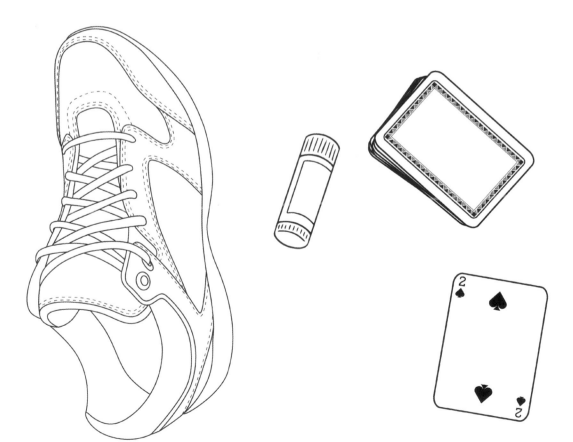

SET-UP

1. To prepare for the effect you'll need to create a special gimmick that will both force a card on a participant and secretly cause it to vanish from the deck. To do this, cut a 1cm strip of the long edge of the extra Two of Spades.

2. Apply glue to the back of this card.

3. Adhere the duplicate Two of Spades to the Joker as shown in the picture. From the front it appears like a normal Joker. On the back, it looks like the Two is lying on the back of the joker. You may want to trim the corners of the card to make sure they are all rounded.

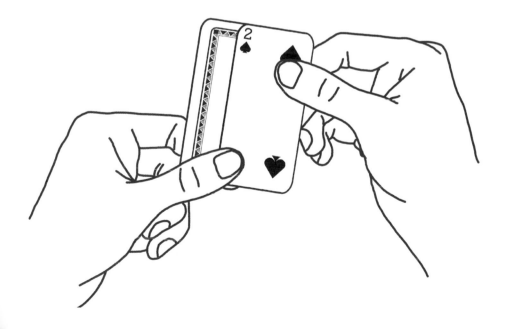

4. Place the other Two of Spades face down in your right shoe. If the card doesn't fit easily, fold it into quarters. Put your shoe back on.

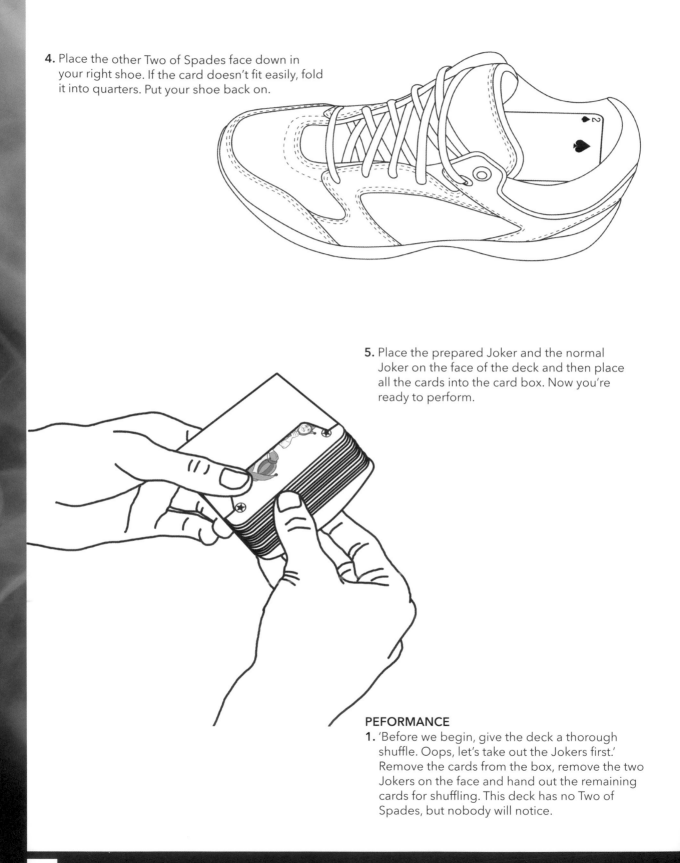

5. Place the prepared Joker and the normal Joker on the face of the deck and then place all the cards into the card box. Now you're ready to perform.

PEFORMANCE

1. 'Before we begin, give the deck a thorough shuffle. Oops, let's take out the Jokers first.' Remove the cards from the box, remove the two Jokers on the face and hand out the remaining cards for shuffling. This deck has no Two of Spades, but nobody will notice.

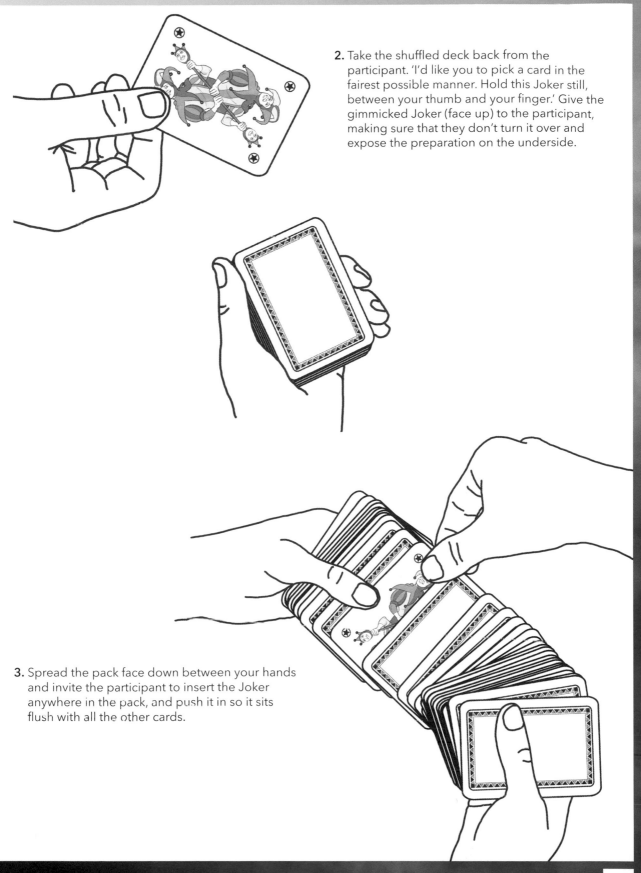

2. Take the shuffled deck back from the participant. 'I'd like you to pick a card in the fairest possible manner. Hold this Joker still, between your thumb and your finger.' Give the gimmicked Joker (face up) to the participant, making sure that they don't turn it over and expose the preparation on the underside.

3. Spread the pack face down between your hands and invite the participant to insert the Joker anywhere in the pack, and push it in so it sits flush with all the other cards.

4. Slowly raise the spread to chest height so the participant can see the faces of the cards. Ask her to remember the card just beneath the Joker. This, of course, will show as the Two of Spades.

With your left fingers, you can tap the face of the Two to emphasize which card he is to remember. This helps ensure they see and remember the force card.

5. Lower the spread back to waist height and remove the Joker (now face up again) from the spread. Place the Joker into your pocket. It won't be used anymore, and you don't want to risk someone picking it up after the effect. (This amazing gimmick not only helped you force the Two of Spades, but also secretly removes it from the deck.)

6. Hand the pack back to the participant. Now mime the action of reaching toward the pack and invisibly extracting one card; you don't actually do anything, but you pretend to remove the card invisibly. Then "throw" this invisible card downward, in the general direction of your feet.

7. 'For the first time aloud, say which card you selected.' He will announce the Two of Spades. Invite him to check in the deck to make sure it's gone, and it is.

8. Show both hands empty and then dramatically remove your right shoe. Reach inside and slowly reveal a face-down card. Turn it over to prove you extracted the card invisibly and made it appear in your shoe!

WITH THANKS TO: The gimmicked card is the invention of one of magic's most creative inventors: Lubor Fiedler. It's called Fiedler's Flyer and you can use it to force and vanish a card for any number of effects. You're not limited to making the card appear in your shoe (although I think that's an unusual, memorable place). You can make it appear under a tablecloth, in your wallet, in a friend's pocket, or anywhere you can hide the card.

MAY THE FORCES BE WITH YOU

This trick uses a force, but so do many others. Throughout this book you have learned several card forces and the cool thing is that they are completely interchangeable. You've learned:

1. The Cross-Cut Force (see 'H2Ooooo', p.28 and 'Magician's Assistant', p.108)

2. The Turnover Force (see 'Instant Kings', p.142)

3. Cut Deeper Force (see 'See-Through', p.102)

4. The Fiedler's Flyer force from this trick

I encourage you to try out all these forces and see which is your favourite!

CHEATING AT BLACKJACK

EFFECT

Ever wanted to cheat in a casino? This is the next best thing – and you never even touch the deck. You ask a participant to shuffle a deck of cards and then bet them some money that you'll beat them at a game of Blackjack. They deal out a hand of two cards each and you win with a perfect 21: an Ace and a King! You offer to repeat it, this time upping the stakes, and you win again.

The best magic has a hook. In this case, you pretend that you can cheat at cards without ever touching the deck. Who doesn't want to win money?

OVERVIEW

It's really simple: you secretly add the winning Blackjack hand to the top of the deck by hiding it under a banknote. It's like a magical Trojan horse!

NEEDED

- A pack of cards
- A wallet
- Two banknotes that are wider than a playing card

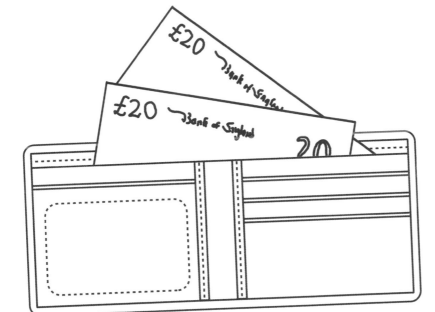

PERFORMANCE

1. Before you perform, you need to remove some cards from the deck. Take out the Ace, Two and King of Spades and put the three cards in that order face down under a banknote. Put the note (with the cards secretly underneath) inside your wallet. The Ace and King will be your winning Blackjack hand and the Two will form part of your participant's losing hand!

If you want to perform the effect twice (many great effects are better if you repeat them, and this one is no exception), simply place the Ace, Two and King of Hearts under a second banknote and put that in a separate section of your wallet.

2. To perform, bring out the remainder of the deck and ask your participant to shuffle it. As they are doing that, claim that you think you can cheat at Blackjack even when the cards are in their hand. If they don't know the rules of the game you can briefly explain that you get two cards each and that the aim of the game is to get the closest to a total of 21 when the value of your hand is added up (Aces can be one or 11 and court cards are always ten). You won't be dealing more than two cards per person so there's no need to explain the intricacies of the game!

3. When they have finished shuffling, ask that they place the deck face down on to the table. Take out your wallet and say, 'I am so confident that I can win the game, I'll even bet you some money!' Remove one of the banknotes while hiding the three cards beneath it by placing your thumb on top and your fingers below (secretly pinning the three cards to the bottom of the note). Make sure that the cards don't peek out from under the banknote, and angle the note downward so that you don't accidentally show that the cards are underneath. Without delay, place the money on top of the deck so that the cards secretly get added to the top.

4. Say, 'And we'll make it even harder for me to cheat – you can hold the money and the deck the entire time.' Ask your participant to pick up the cards and to place the money to one side for a moment. The deck is now stacked so that you'll always win. The participant must simply follow the Blackjack game by dealing a card to you, then a card to themselves, then one to you again and then one back to themselves. Say, 'Please put the cards down on to the table so that nobody can accuse you of switching the cards!' (Really they're putting the cards onto the table so that you can add more cards to it if you repeat the effect!)

5. Let them turn over their two cards. You don't know exactly what they will get, but the Two that you snuck on to the deck under the banknote means that it won't be a good hand! At best it will be 13, which won't beat the 21 that they have unknowingly given you.

6. Finally, turn over your cards and show that you have a perfect Blackjack! Quickly take your banknote back and celebrate that you won the game.

7. If you put another banknote into your wallet before the effect, we'll now repeat it. Take out the other note (with the cards hidden underneath) and put it on top of the deck, along with the first banknote, and say, 'OK, one last time – this time I'll even double my bet!' You can now perform the exact effect again, and once again, you'll win!

LET THE MAGIC BREATHE

Watching yourself on television is a surreal experience, but it can also be brutal. Not many of us ever get the opportunity to watch ourselves interact, speak and perform magic. One thing I learned early on is that as magicians, we don't often appreciate just how special our magic can be. We rush the moment. Don't do this.

Let your magic breathe. Let people enjoy the best part of any effect: the magic! Pause briefly before the moment of magic to increase the drama, and let the audience speak or think or enjoy what they're feeling at the end of the performance. This is the reason that I often walk away at the end of a performance!

You'll know when the moment is right to perform another effect, or thank them and move on. But if you've worked hard on a new effect, remember to let the magic breathe.

CATCH

EFFECT
You show two cards, and then insert them very fairly into the middle of the deck. You then throw the deck from one hand to the other, and somehow you manage to catch the two cards between your hands.

However modern an effect looks, it is always always built on hundreds of years of mysteries. This one uses magic principles from centuries ago, yet still fools everyone I show it to! Due to the clever principle used (magicians call it a mis-show), this effect is incredibly easy to do. Follow along with a deck of cards and you'll be able to do it straight away.

OVERVIEW
The two cards that you show are actually different to the two cards you produce. But the cards that you show and the cards that you produce are so similar that the audience always confuse them.

NEEDED
A pack of cards

SET-UP
Before you start, there's a little secret preparation to do. Remove the Six of Hearts and Nine of Diamonds from the deck and put them to one side. Also remove the Nine of Hearts and Six of Diamonds and place one of them on top of the deck and the other on the bottom.

PERFORMANCE
1. Show the two cards that you placed aside and say, 'We'll use these two red cards for this next effect: the red Six and Nine.' It's important not to tell people the suits of the cards here. Remember I told you people would confuse the cards you use? These are those cards; with a little time delay, your audience will not notice that you are actually swapping the two suits of the cards. This is the mis-show principle. It probably seems obvious now that you know it, but nobody ever notices that they have changed.

2. Spread the deck face down along the table (see the 'ribbon spread' later in the book to learn how to do this).

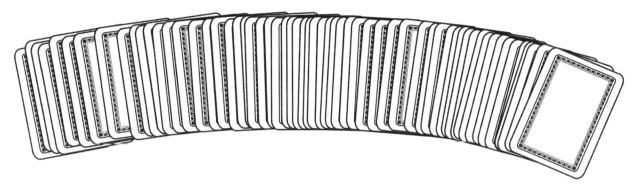

3. Take the red Six and Nine and insert them face down into two different parts of the deck. Sometimes I like to have someone else put the cards into the deck so that they are truly convinced that the cards are lost in the deck.

4. Close the tabled spread and pick up the deck.

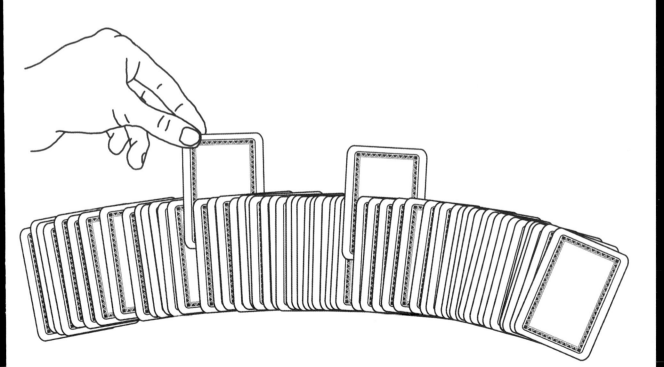

5. For the mis-show to work most effectively, you need to delay the reproduction of the cards so that the audience forget the suits of the Six and Nine. An easy way to do that is to ask someone in the audience: 'Do you remember the exact position in which I put those cards? And could you find them? How about with one hand?' They will say no to all those questions, which helps make the effect even stronger.

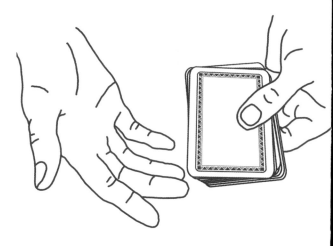

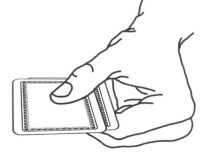

6. Now for the reproduction. Hold the deck in your left hand with your thumb on top and fingers below. Your thumb should be exactly in the middle of the deck and your fingers should be extended underneath.

7. Throw the deck from your left hand to your right hand while pushing down with your thumb. This will cause the top and bottom cards (the other red Six and Nine) to stay in your left hand, while all the other cards are tossed across to your right hand.

8. Put the deck from your right hand on the table. Then turn over the two cards in your left hand and say, 'There we go; the red Six and Nine… with one hand!' Again, don't mention the exact cards, only that they are the red Six and Nine, and your audience will never suspect anything untoward!

ACE CATCH

There's a way of doing this production with the four Aces. Put two Aces on the top and two Aces on the bottom of the deck, and hold the cards exactly as described in Step 6. Now, throw the deck from the left hand to the right, automatically keeping hold of the top and bottom cards as before.

When you catch the deck in your right hand, immediately put your thumb on top, and then throw the deck from the right hand on to the table, pinching the deck in the exact same way as before so that you are left holding the new top and bottom cards of the deck. Turn your hands over to show that you are holding the four Aces.

LIAR

EFFECT

You ask a participant to call out the names of playing cards they see in the pack while you look away, and you invite them to lie to you about which one they picked. You know instantly when they are lying!

Sometimes the secret of a magic effect is even cleverer than you might expect. For example, what if you could know the exact order of a deck of cards without memorising them? That's exactly what you're doing here; and it's very easy to do!

OVERVIEW

The deck is in a secret order known to magicians as the Si Stebbins stack. When the participant names the order of the cards they have taken, you'll be able to know which one they are lying about because it will be the only one that isn't in the correct order.

NEEDED

A pack of cards

SET-UP

First you must set up the deck in a Si Stebbins stack. From the top down, put the cards in this order:

Ace of Clubs	Ace of Spades
Four of Hearts	Four of Diamonds
Seven of Spades	Seven of Clubs
Ten of Diamonds	Ten of Hearts
King of Clubs	King of Spades
Three of Hearts	Three of Diamonds
Six of Spades	Six of Clubs
Nine of Diamonds	Nine of Hearts
Queen of Clubs	Queen of Spades
Two of Hearts	Two of Diamonds
Five of Spades	Five of Clubs
Eight of Diamonds	Eight of Hearts
Jack of Clubs	Jack of Spades
Ace of Hearts	Ace of Diamonds
Four of Spades	Four of Clubs
Seven of Diamonds	Seven of Hearts
Ten of Clubs	Ten of Spades
King of Hearts	King of Diamonds
Three of Spades	Three of Clubs
Six of Diamonds	Six of Hearts
Nine of Clubs	Nine of Spades
Queen of Hearts	Queen of Diamonds
Two of Spades	Two of Clubs
Five of Diamonds	Five of Hearts
Eight of Clubs	Eight of Spades
Jack of Hearts	Jack of Diamonds

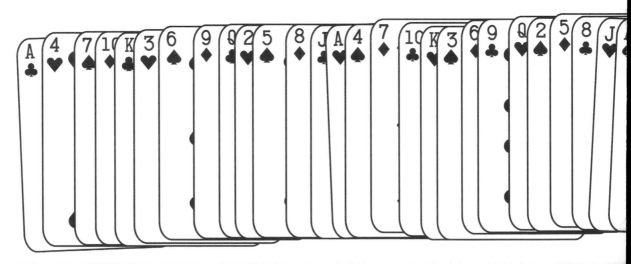

This is a special order that allows you to see one card and then know what the next card is. The best way to learn this system is to remember two rules:

1. The order of the suits is Clubs, Hearts, Spades, then Diamonds. It's easy to remember this by thinking of the acronym CHaSeD (forget the 'a' and the 'e', and the word spells the order of the four suits). This means that if you see a Heart, the suit of the next card will be a Spade. The suits are cyclical, meaning that if you see a Diamond, you go right back to the start and so the next card is a Club.

2. The numbers always go up by three. So, if you see a Two, the next card is a Five, then an Eight. Court cards are 11 (Jack), 12 (Queen) and 13 (King), so after an Eight would be a Jack. The numbers are cyclical too, so if you see a Jack, the card after it is an Ace.

Let's connect that together. Imagine that you cut to the Seven of Spades; the next card in the stack would be the Ten of Diamonds (add three to the value, and go to the next suit in the CHaSeD suit sequence). The card after the Nine of Clubs would be the King of Hearts, and so on. Look at the illustration of the stack and you'll see how it always works.

Remembering those two rules means that you don't have to remember the exact order of the deck. So long as you see one card, you can always calculate the next card in the stack.

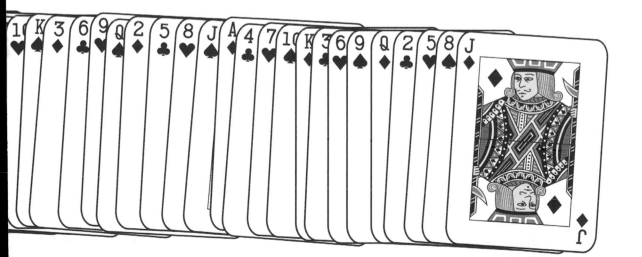

PERFORMANCE:

1. Now that you know the secret to the stack, the effect becomes quite easy. Make sure that the deck is in Si Stebbins order and that you have remembered the two rules to the secret stack.

Ask a participant to cut the deck, and to complete the cut. They can cut as often as they like – it won't ruin the stack.

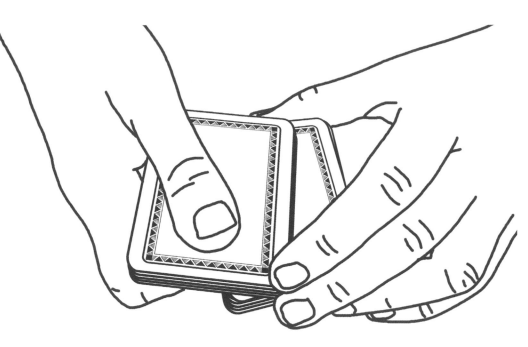

2. When your participant has decided to stop cutting the cards, ask that they cut four or five cards from the top of the deck and then hold them just like they would if they were playing a game of cards.

3. Explain the rules: 'In a moment I am going to turn my back and I would like you to turn over each card, one by one, face up on to the table. Then name your cards out loud as you deal them. But there's a twist: I'd like you to lie about any one of those cards. Just name any other card in the deck, except for the one you see. I'll then try to use my secret powers to pick up on which card you lied about.' Turn your back and ask them to start dealing (you might need to remind them of the rules while they deal the first couple of cards).

4. All you need to do now is listen and follow along. Start with the first card they name and follow with the Si Stebbins sequence that you just learned. Whichever card they name doesn't fit with the rules, you know is the card that they have lied about. But here's the best thing: using the Si Stebbins sequence, you can even tell them the actual card.

That's the method, but we really must add some presentation. So instead of just naming the card the participant lied about, I suggest saying something like, 'People tend to find lying uncomfortable and I think you do, too. That's why you hesitated before lying about the card. You named the Six of Hearts but that was a lie. The card you should have named was the Two of Diamonds!'

BLIND LUCK

EFFECT
You test your compatibility with someone else by each taking half the deck under the table and selecting a card for each other. When you look at your cards, you have both selected red Queens!

How do you make a great impression with magic? You perform it for the right person at the right time! Here's a very easy effect created by my friend Andi Gladwin that I think would be perfect to perform for someone you're trying to attract, as the central theme is that of you magically finding matching cards for each other.

OVERVIEW
Performing the effect under the table is a great conceit as it means that you can do absolutely anything with the cards, without the participant seeing. In this case, you're switching the card that the participant selected for one that you want them to pick!

NEEDED
A pack of cards

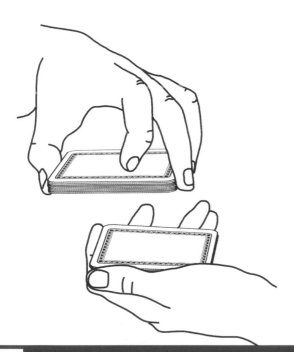

SET-UP
- Place the two red Queens on the bottom of the deck.
- Ideally sit opposite your participant so that you can look directly into their eyes. You'll need a table to perform on.

PERFORMANCE
1. Hold the deck face down in your hand and ask your participant to cut off approximately half the cards. (This leaves you with the bottom half of the deck with the two Queens on the bottom of your packet.)

2. Ask that they take their cards below the table, and do the same with your cards.

3. Then ask them to look you straight in the eyes and without looking at the cards, spread through the deck until they get to a card that they like. Talk slowly and encourage them throughout as it's surprisingly difficult to spread the cards and remove one without being able to look at your hands.

4. Tell them to square their cards in their right hand and to hold their selection in their left hand.

5. Ask them to hand you their card (still under the table) and explain that you'll pick a card and give it to them. Actually, you give them the bottom card of your packet, pretending that you took it from the middle.

6. Tell them to turn over the card you just gave them and to insert it face up into their packet.

7. You'll apparently do the same, but in reality you'll do something quite different. Take the card they gave you and put it on top of your packet. Then take the bottom card of your packet, turn it over and insert it into the middle of your cards too. As all this happens under the table the participant will just assume that you put the selected card in the deck.

8. Both bring your packets above the table and spread them out. You'll both find that you have reversed red Queens! A perfect match!

PART 3
SKILLS 101

When you perform magic, you often have less than ten seconds to establish yourself before people lose interest, or worse, walk away. This final chapter contains no magic, but has amazing flourishes and demonstrations of skill and dexterity that will impress any audience.

While many magicians don't consider 'flourishing' (an open display of skill) to be magic, I think that it's magical and shows that you can do almost anything with a deck of cards or a coin. It's a great way to make an instant good impression!

COIN ROLL

This was one of the first coin moves that I learned. It's not an effect, but a skilful way of manipulating a coin or poker chip over your knuckles. It is by far the hardest move in this book, but is really fun to practise – I still work on it regularly to keep my fingers nimble! Magicians call this kind of move a flourish and I think it's one of the things that audiences enjoy watching.

NEEDED

A big coin or poker chip. I typically use a £2 coin or a 50p piece as the bigger the coin, the easier the flourish is.

1. Start by curling your right hand into a loose fist. The exact position of the hand doesn't matter at this stage but I prefer to hold it with my thumb closest to my body and the little finger facing the audience.

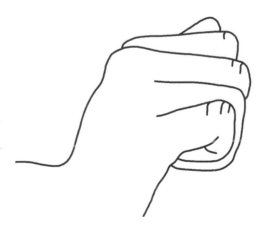

2. Take your coin and place it so that it is held between your thumb and first finger. Try to have the coin extend as far over the fingers as possible. The more it protrudes, the easier the move is.

3. Release your thumb's grip on the coin, allowing it to automatically fall over, end-for-end, flat on to your first finger.

4. Without pausing, raise your second finger up slightly and then lower it down directly on to the edge of the coin, causing the coin to stand on edge again (but this time pinched between the first and second fingers). Throughout the entire move, your hand is kept in a loose fist and the coin has moved with only very slight movements of the fingers.

5. Just like before, loosen your grip on the coin, and this time it will fall forward on to the second finger. Raise the second finger and lower it back on to the edge of the coin, so that you now pinch it between the second and third fingers.

6. Repeat these exact actions again until you have the coin pinched between your third and little fingers. Obviously this will take some practice, but it's really fun to do. The more momentum the coin gets up, the easier it becomes and eventually the coin will roll down your knuckles in just a couple of seconds.

7. You must now move the coin back to its starting position. Reach your right thumb under your right hand and let the coin slide gently down between your third and little fingers until it rests flatly on the right thumb.

8. Very carefully move your thumb backward and up against the side of your first finger, pinning the coin to your hand just like at the very start of the move. During this sequence try not to flatten your hand – I believe it looks much nicer if the hand stays in a loose fist.

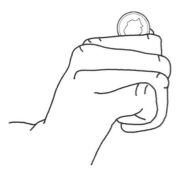

9. Repeat the move again… and again… and again. It looks great when it's in full motion! When I first learned it, I tried to practise it about 50 times per day. My big tip is to practise it over a bed so that it doesn't make a big noise when you drop the coin (and you'll drop it a lot to start with!).

CARD THROWING

It's time to be a magic ninja! Over the past two centuries magicians have perfected card-throwing techniques in interesting ways: Rick Smith, Jr. holds the current world record for throwing a card the farthest and fastest with a throw that was 65.96 metres long and 91.96 mph! Another magician, Ricky Jay, can throw a card from across the room with such force and accuracy that it pierces a watermelon. The technique I use was invented by Alexander Herrmann, who was probably the first magician to throw cards in his show, back in the 1800s. That's the one we'll teach here:

1. First we must look at how to hold the card, as knowing the correct grip is the secret to throwing the card a long way. Take a single card and hold it, face down, so that it is parallel to the floor in your right hand, with your first finger extending along the front end of the card so that it reaches all the way across the card. Place your second finger underneath the card, and your thumb on top. That exact grip is vital to throwing the card a long way.

NEEDED
A single card

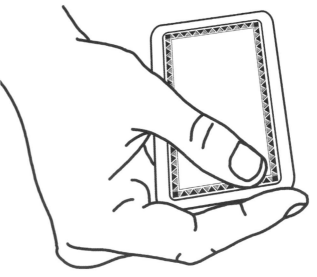

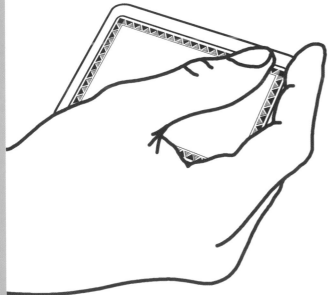

2. Bend your wrist inward so that the bottom right corner of the card contacts your wrist. This is your starting position.

3. To throw the card, flick your wrist forward, keeping your arm as straight as possible (this will, in turn, keep the card straight and parallel to the floor). As you flick your wrist, let go of the card, causing it to propel itself forward. The power comes from this flick of your wrist, so focus on flicking it out really hard.

You can also extend your arm as you flick the wrist forward to help create extra distance, but for the best results you must work on propelling the card by flicking the wrist.

That's the basic technique. But like all good sleight of hand, it requires practice. Get an old deck and keep practising it; the more practice you put in, the farther and harder you'll be able to throw the card.

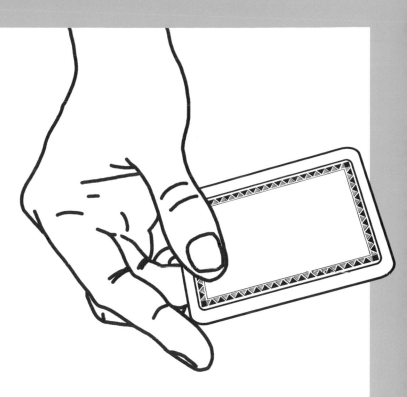

CARDS AS WEAPONS?

Several television shows, movies and computer games have shown playing cards being used as an impromptu weapon, and there has even been a book written on the subject. But can they really be used to cause harm?

First of all: please don't actually throw a card at someone in case it hits them in the eye! But it turns out that even when thrown by a machine that can fire a card almost twice as fast a person, the worst damage a card can do to human skin is give it a paper cut! Cards just don't weigh enough to be used as actual weapons… but I'll continue to practise throwing them just in case!

PENDULUM CUT

EFFECT

It looks as if you mix the cards in a fancy, complex way, but actually you don't shuffle the cards at all.

A lot of people know me for my 'Dynamo Shuffle'. That shuffle is what magicians refer to as a flourish, and it's part of a movement called Cardistry. The ones I do take years of practice, but I began with flourishes like this one, so it's the perfect one for you to start with. You may wish to throw in the Pendulum Cut when you perform the other effects I teach. It will help convince the audience that the cards aren't stacked in a particular order (even when they are).

OVERVIEW

Although you will divide the deck into several packets, you assemble them in the same order in which they began.

NEEDED

A pack of cards

PERFORMANCE

1. Hold the pack in your right hand, from above. The right fingers rest on the outer end of the pack and the thumb braces the deck from the inner end.

2. With your first finger, lift up a third of the deck, breaking the deck into two packets.

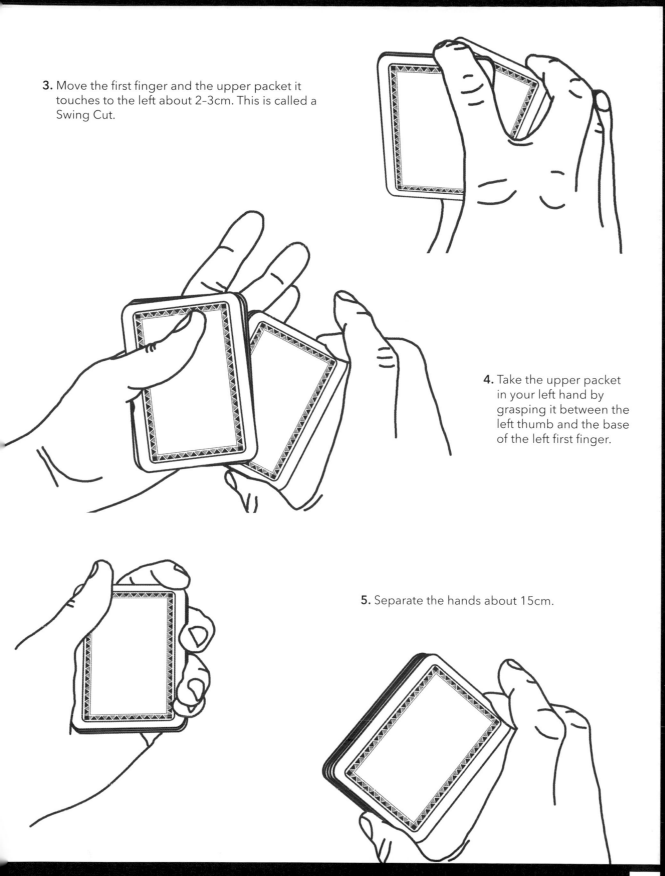

3. Move the first finger and the upper packet it touches to the left about 2–3cm. This is called a Swing Cut.

4. Take the upper packet in your left hand by grasping it between the left thumb and the base of the left first finger.

5. Separate the hands about 15cm.

6. Repeat Step 2, once again breaking the right-hand packet in two by lifting half of the cards upward with your right first finger.

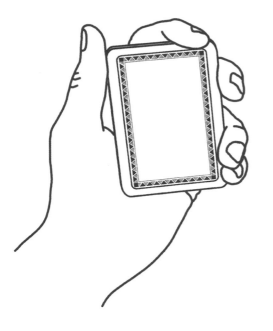

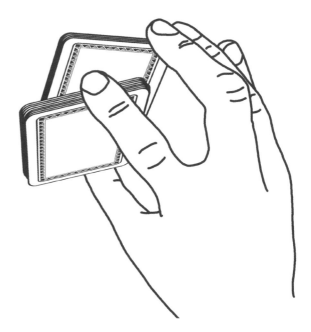

7. Rotate the right wrist so the right thumb is uppermost.

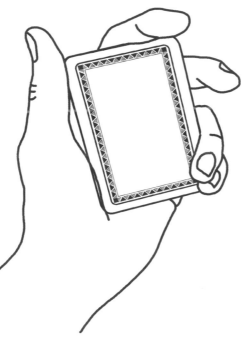

8. With your left second finger and thumb, grasp the lowermost packet in your right hand. The left second finger and thumb can take hold of this packet despite the cards they already hold. At first it may seem impossible to keep track of three separate packets, but it becomes easier with practice.

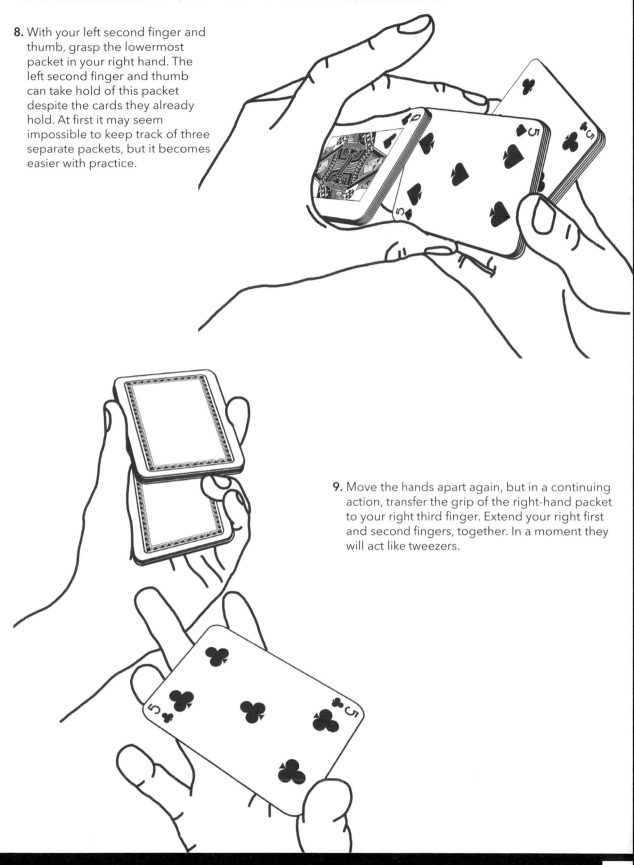

9. Move the hands apart again, but in a continuing action, transfer the grip of the right-hand packet to your right third finger. Extend your right first and second fingers, together. In a moment they will act like tweezers.

10. Take the lower packet held in your left hand between the right first and second fingers. Pinch this packet by turning the right wrist upward again and placing your second finger on top of the left hand's lower packet, at the same time placing your right first finger beneath the packet.

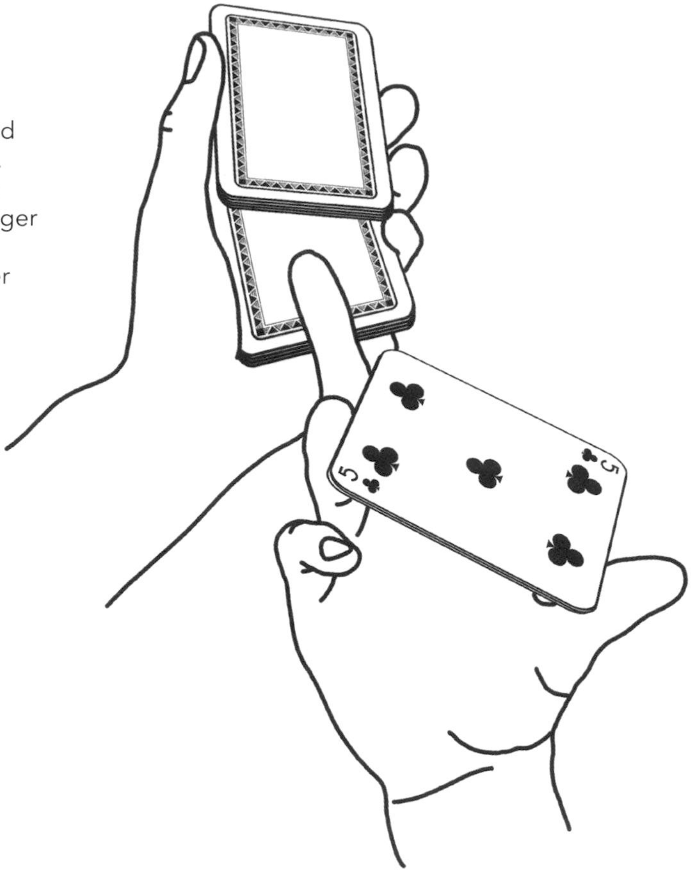

11. As you slide this packet out toward your body. Turn your right hand palm side down.

12. Now it's time to put everything back together (and secretly, you will place each packet back in exactly the order they started in). Place the packet held in your right hand between the right thumb and fingers on top of the cards in your left hand.

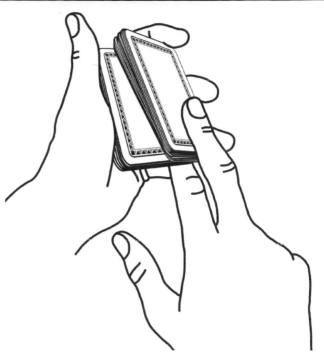

13. To conclude, place the cards pinched between your right first and second fingers face down on top of everything.

Despite all this mixing, the cards are still in their original order. Practise the Pendulum Cut over and over until you can do it quickly and without looking at your hands.

WITH THANKS TO: Troy Hooser is a magician from the USA who helped create some influential flourishes. This one is that rare kind of flourish that is easy to do but looks impressive when done quickly.

RIBBON SPREAD AND TURNOVER

Spreading cards on the table is an easy flourish that shows that you mean business at the card table! Once you have learned the basic spread, you can then add the turnover flourish, which really takes things up a level. You must perform this flourish on a soft surface like a card table, a bed or a carpet because it doesn't work well on hard, slippery surfaces.

NEEDED
A pack of cards

RIBBON SPREAD

1. Hold the face-down deck in your right hand at the short ends with your thumb at the back and your fingers at the front. Move your first finger to the left long side of the deck.

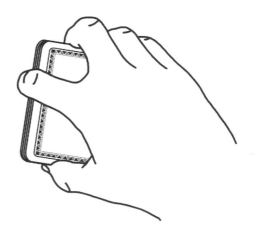

2. Lower the deck to the table, reaching your hand across your body to the left. This is the starting point of the spread.

3. Apply a little downward pressure with your right hand as you pull the hand from left to right. This will cause the cards to create a nice spread along the table. The cards may initially clump together, but with practice, you can create a really uniform-looking spread. While you can make the spread as wide as a metre or so, the ideal length to practise with is about 30–40cm. This way, the cards are close enough together to allow you to continue on to the turnover.

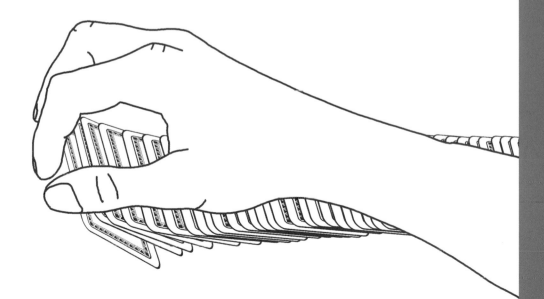

TURNOVER
4. Dig your left fingers under the left end of the spread (the bottom of the deck).

5. Raise your left hand so that the cards at that end of the spread are raised up, on their ends.

6. Lower your left thumb on to the long edge of the raised cards.

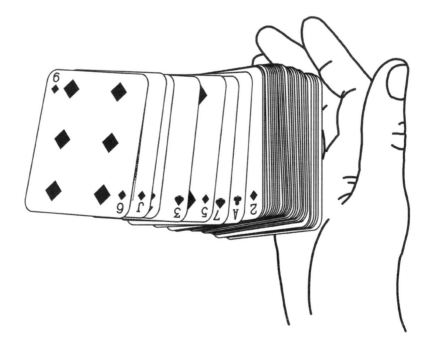

7. Drag your left thumb along the spread, causing the cards to turn over slowly. Stop when you reach the end of the spread, when the entire deck is face up.

If you find that the spread separated during the turnover it is likely due to one of three issues: the deck is too old and warped (a new deck is best), your spread was too wide or the surface you are using is too hard. With this in mind, keep practising and you'll eventually perform the perfect ribbon spread and turnover!

RIFFLE SHUFFLE

Being able to thoroughly shuffle cards on a table is an important skill if you wish to get serious about card magic. This is how they shuffle cards in Las Vegas.

NEEDED
A pack of cards

1. Begin with the pack on the table in front of you with the sides aligned with the table's edge.

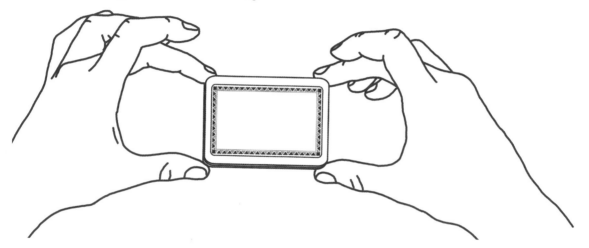

2. Grasp the top half of the deck near the right corners between your right thumb and fingers.

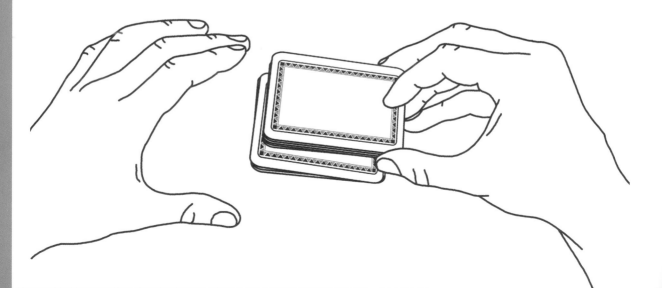

3. Lift up the top half of the deck and place these cards to the right of the lower packet, about an inch apart.

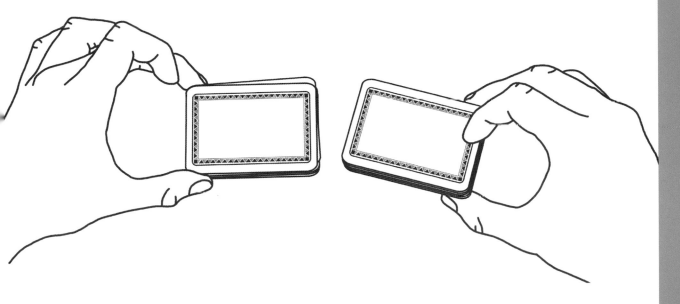

4. Grasp the two packets, one in each hand, from above. Position your thumbs at the inner corners of each packet, bracing them from the outer corners with the first and second fingertips.

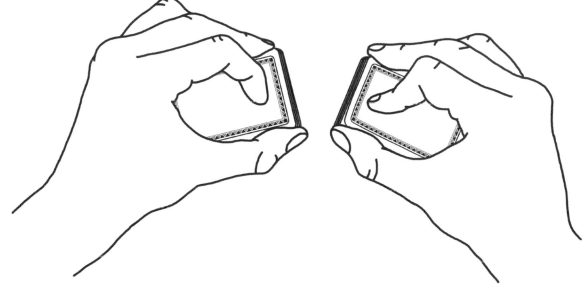

5. Move the inner corners toward each other, so that the right packet's inner left corner is almost touching the left packet's inner right corner.

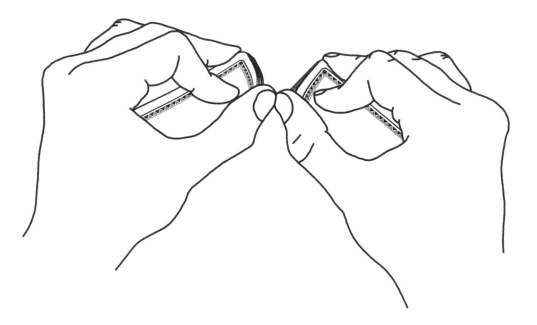

6. Riffle the cards from each packet off your thumbs so that the cards interlace. When you first begin, the cards may riffle off in clumps. But as you refine your technique, you should be able to riffle the cards fluidly one by one.

7. After the cards have been interlaced, release your grip for a moment, allowing the cards to rest on the table in a partially mixed condition.

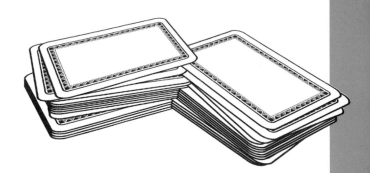

8. Reposition your hands on the tabled packets from above, with your little fingers bracing the packets at their outer ends.

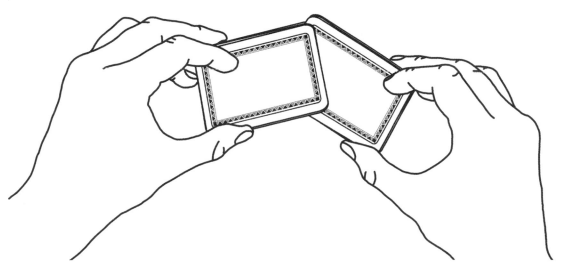

9. Bring the cards together by pushing the packets into each other, using all of your fingers to entirely square the cards.

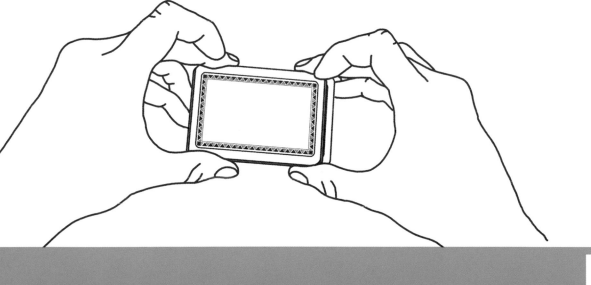

CARD FAN

This is a classic flourish in which you show all the faces of the cards to be different. You'll need a newer, high-quality deck of cards to make a fan that is smooth. Older cards will tend to clump together as you're trying to fan them.

NEEDED
A pack of cards

1. Begin by holding the cards face up from above in your right hand. Place them in your left hand, wedged tightly in the webbing at the base of your left thumb.

2. Place your right first finger on the left side of the pack, near the upper left corner.

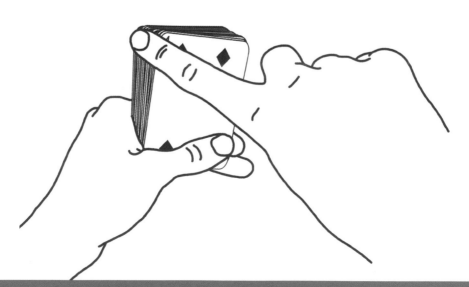

3. Move your first finger in a large, clockwise, circular direction, smearing the cards into a fan. You have to hold the pack in your left hand quite lightly to allow the cards to spread.

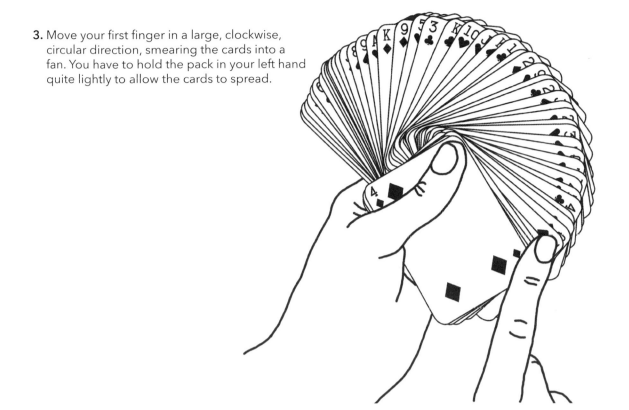

4. Practise spreading the cards into the largest possible fan, and aim to get an even distribution of space between each card. A fast first-finger motion is your best chance to get an even, attractive fan.

5. You may wish to fan the cards face down in your left hand so that after the fan is complete you can raise it to chest height and display the faces outward, next to your face. No corny posing here, please.

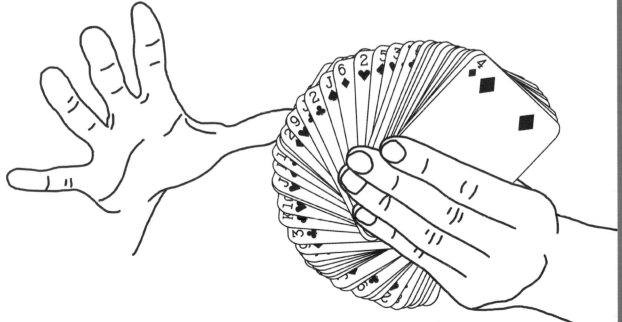

OUTRO

When you start in magic, performing your first illusion feels like the end of a journey. Actually, this is just your first step into a larger world. Magic only begins in front of an audience. The biggest tip I can offer you for your magical journey is this: listen to your audience. Their reactions will tell you what works and what needs work. If they catch you out (and it happens to all of us), you'll know exactly what you need to do next time. Whenever I'm in doubt, I just remind myself to let the audience guide my material.

I hope this glimpse into my mind has inspired you to pursue magic. If it has, these are some great next steps:

VOLUNTEER

I promise you this: your first show will be great fun, but probably not your finest hour. That's okay! It's part of the process of improving and learning as a magician. This is why I suggest that you volunteer for charities, retirement centres or anywhere that your magic will brighten an audience's day. These audiences are often starved of entertainment, and they will appreciate even your earliest efforts.

PRACTISE EVERY DAY

If practising magic feels like a drag, this feeling will pass as you get better at it. You have to learn to love rehearsing, learning new magic and practising the same movements and script over and over until they're perfect. For me, practice is like my meditation; it's how I start every day, and how I unwind every evening.

JOIN A MAGIC CLUB

There are magic clubs all around the country. If you're under 18, The Young Magicians Club (**www.youngmagiciansclub.co.uk**) is a great club to help you develop your magic skills. If you're over 18, The Magic Circle (**www.themagiccircle.co.uk**) is worth considering too as your passion for magic grows.

Magic has changed my life for ever. My sincere hope is that magic can do the same for you.

CREDITS
Quote: p 20 - 21 from Billy and the Minpins by Roald Dahl, published by Puffin Books. Reproduced by permission of David Higham Associates Ltd.
Photography: p.2: Andrew Timms; p.11: Andrew Timms; p.26 - 27: Andrew Timms; p.38 – 39: Andrew Timms; p.57: Shutterstock; p.65: Kevin Mazur/Getty Images; p.70 - 71: Andrew Timms; p.100 - 101: Andrew Timms; p.147: Andrew Timms; p.191: Thomas Smyth; p.192: Andrew Timms

Acknowledgements: Dan Albion, Thomas Smyth, Clare Britt, Harry De Cruz, Tom Elderfield, Andi Gladwin, Joshua Jay, George Luck, Tommaso Di Filippo, Marc Kerstein, David Pitt, Asif Rahman, Andre Etienne, Andrew Timms, Richard Johnson, Kelly Ellis & everyone at Bonnier Publishing, The Magic Circle, Dawbell PR